STUDENTS OF HOSPITALFIELD

STUDENTS OF HOSPITALFIELD
Education and Inspiration in 20th-Century Scottish Art

Peggy Beardmore

Sansom &
Company

First published in 2018 by Sansom and Company,
a publishing imprint of Redcliffe Press Ltd.
81G Pembroke Road, Bristol BS8 3EA
www.sansomandcompany.co.uk • info@sansomandcompany.co.uk

ISBN 978-1-911408-23-9

British Library Cataloguing-in-Publication Data
A catalogue record for this book is available from the British Library

Design and typesetting by E&P Design
Printed by Cambrian Print Ltd

Cover: James Cowie, *Studio Interior*, 1946–7
Frontispiece: Hospitalfield House as viewed from the garden,
photograph © Ruth Clark, image courtesy of Hospitalfield, 2017

Contents

Acknowledgements

This book was made possible through the generosity of the late artist, teacher and student of Hospitalfield Joan Cuthill, whose bequest to the Hospitalfield Alumni Association funded its research. Many thanks to the Hospitalfield Alumni Association and the History of Art Department of the University of Aberdeen, whose partnership was essential to its creation, with particular thanks to Mae McKenzie Smith, Chair of the Hospitalfield Alumni Association and to my supervisors Dr John Morrison and Dr Mary Pryor.

A great deal of thanks is due to the many individuals and organisations that have been instrumental in this research coming to fruition. Hospitalfield: Director Lucy Byatt, Programme and Facilities Manager Laura Simpson and General Manager Scott Byrne. Elphinstone Institute, University of Aberdeen: Director Dr Tom McKean and Archivist Nicolas Le Bigre. The Royal Scottish Academy of Art and Architecture, Glasgow School of Art, University of Edinburgh, University of Dundee and Arbroath Art Society for consultation of archival material. Hunterian Art Gallery, National Galleries of Scotland, University of Abertay, Glenalmond College, Robert Gordon University, Fife Contemporary Art and Craft and The National Library of Scotland for answering enquiries. Special thanks to the Scottish Society for Art History for their research grant, which allowed me to access material at the British Library.

An immense amount of gratitude is due to those who so willingly shared their experiences of Hospitalfield: Claire Ashley, Allan Beveridge, Joyce Cairns, Bill Connon, George Donald, Lennox Dunbar, Alistair Fleming and Elspeth Macpherson (née Fleming), Susan Forsyth, Alexander Fraser, Morris Grassie, Gwen Hardie, Eugeniusz Jarych, Susan Kraut, David Lockhart, Will Maclean, Jean Martin, Ella McCalman, Ian McCulloch, Joe McIntyre, Ian McKenzie Smith, Mae McKenzie Smith, Alastair MacLennan, James Morrison, Dawson Murray, Ann Patrick, Alan Robb, Hugh Robertson, Janet Tod, Frances Walker and Kate Whiteford. Thanks also to Neil Allan, Jane Bannister and Jim Gallacher, Mark Campbell, Ruth Christie, Martin Fowler, Jane Furst and Beryl Gascoigne, Andrew Grassie, Raymond Lafferty, Gillian Mather, Robert McNeill, Kristin Mojsiewicz, Ian Richie, Susan Smith and Helen Wilson for the correspondence and images that illuminated Hospitalfield's history. Lastly, I would like to thank my husband, Michael, for his love and support throughout this process as well as my family, friends and teachers for their belief in me over the years.

Introduction

Today, the house and surrounding grounds of Hospitalfield in Arbroath still retain a sense of the evocative power that made such an impression on Charles Robert Swift. To the modern reader, his reflections may seem overly nostalgic or romantic, yet they are indicative of the significance of his encounter with Hospitalfield fifty years earlier, when he enrolled there as one of the first students at the newly founded Allan-Fraser Art College. There is also a resonance in them that surpasses time. Speak to anyone who has spent time at Hospitalfield and there is likely to be a similar sense of wonder, curiosity and awe that weaves its way through their descriptions of the place and their experiences there. What is indicated by Swift's reminiscences, these descriptions and the support that led to this research being produced, is that there is something special about this house and estate in the northeast of Scotland.

Look in the index of books about Scottish art and architecture, and the name 'Hospitalfield' will likely be listed. It frequently appears in relation to Patrick Allan-Fraser, the artist and philanthropist who was its last private owner, the Allan-Fraser Art College (1890–1935) that his bequest founded, or the Patrick Allan-Fraser Trust Scheme (1935–94) administered by Scotland's four art schools in Aberdeen, Dundee, Edinburgh and Glasgow. Go to the referred page number, however, and often only a few relevant paragraphs or even as little as a single sentence will appear. Although, together, these passages provide some insight into Hospitalfield's history, their brevity reveals that there is much that has not been written. Similarly, Hospitalfield has long been a recognisable name within Scotland's arts community, but little known by the public beyond. Even those familiar with it were often unaware of the full extent of its importance and legacy. Hospitalfield's twentieth century is, therefore, a recent history whose meaning and significance was hidden in plain sight.

Drawing from archival material, newly recorded oral history interviews and the artwork of public and private collections, this first dedicated study of Hospitalfield's significance in the development of twentieth-century Scottish art explores the amazing trajectory that led Hospitalfield to transform from a home into an art school into an essential part of Scottish art education.

Consulting archival records proved essential to establishing a twentieth-century chronology of events at Hospitalfield and beginning to understand the breadth of their impact. The distribution of these archival records among several institutions – including Hospitalfield, the Royal Scottish Academy of Art and Architecture, Edinburgh College of Art and Glasgow School of Art – also reflects the breadth of its influence. In addition, it demonstrates the ways in which Hospitalfield's art school and, later, artist residency programme, was embedded within the fabric of Scotland's art and art educational infrastructure for nearly a century.

Lastly, it is emblematic of the shared nature of Hospitalfield's history. As the site of the Allan-Fraser Art College and the Patrick Allan-Fraser Trust Scheme, Hospitalfield acted as an interchange, a junction. It was a place to which artists came with their skills and affinities. These developed, expanded and were exchanged within a creative community.

The impact of these new experiences then continued to evolve with the development of the artists' careers. This progression has meant that, throughout the twentieth century, the Hospitalfield experience has connected something in the region of 700 artists of different generations and locales, each possessing diverse outlooks and artistic practices.[2]

'Hospitalfield: I have never lost the pleasure of those early days when the celestial, heaven born music of the warbling birds, the rustling of the trees and the distant swirling of the waves on the seashore beyond the South Drive, came floating on the scented air all around, holding all heaven and earth in happy union ... Here is a fairy-land in which visitors may find themselves transported, as in a dream, from the earth they have known as all commonplace. A spot rendered sacred by associations historic and romantic, which will excite the highest degree of respect and reverence from those who visit it.'[1]

CHARLES ROBERT SWIFT

Entrance to Hospitalfield House, Hospitalfield, Arbroath

The effect that the Hospitalfield experience had upon its students is therefore at the core of its significance. These students include the young artists who attended the Allan-Fraser Art College as well as those who were selected by the art schools to participate in the Patrick Allan-Fraser Trust Scheme. They also include those artists who engaged with Hospitalfield at a more mature point in their career, as Governor, Warden, or artist in residence – who, as students of the place, learned from and responded to the visual environment and community of artists at Hospitalfield.

For these artists, Hospitalfield exists within a personal history. Oral history interviews now archived in the University of Aberdeen's Elphinstone Institute, as well as conversations and correspondences with past participants, have provided insight into the nature of Hospitalfield's arts programming and its individual significance, much of which illuminates its broader significance for the collective of artists who participated in that programming. Excerpts of the interviews are therefore featured throughout the text so that the artists' own words about the profound meaning of their experiences at Hospitalfield could be shared.

The content and structure of this book has been inspired by the archival and oral sources that informed it. The chapter divisions, which correspond

with consistencies in Hospitalfield's mission as an educational establishment and the leaders who guided it, have been based upon the archival sources (such as meeting minutes, governance documents and accounts) that outlined the story of how Hospitalfield's ever-changing mission was continuously redirected by the cultural contexts and personal visions of those who owned, cared for and inhabited it. The institutional perspective that these documents provide is then complemented by the oral histories, which share the reflections of those who experienced Hospitalfield's institutional aims in action. Oral history and the artworks themselves offer insight into what exactly defined the Hospitalfield experience and why, if or how it was important. More specifically, these accounts speak to the opportunities Hospitalfield gave for personal and artistic growth, the exchange of ideas with new-found friends and contemporaries, and artistic engagement with its diverse visual environment. These motifs continuously reappear in each chapter to reveal aspects of cohesion within what is, otherwise, a convoluted history.

In the twenty-first century, the mission and significance of the charitable trust Hospitalfield continues to evolve as it engages with artists, writers, scholars and the public in new ways. It is, therefore, timely that just as this institution grows toward a new future vision, there is pause for reflection to examine, question, consider and celebrate the significance Hospitalfield has had within the development of Scottish art and education in the twentieth century.

1

A new vision
for Hospitalfield

The estate located outside the town centre of Arbroath, known as Hospitalfield, has served a variety of purposes through time. Its name refers to
its fourteenth-century function as a pilgrim hospice for the Arbroath Abbey,
founded in 1178 by William I. In the days of the Abbey, Arbroath was a seat
of political and religious power. Today, it is perhaps best known as the site
of the Declaration of Arbroath (1320), a document which eloquently and
passionately argued for Scotland's independence. The Reformation, however,
brought about dramatic social, religious and cultural change in the sixteenth
century. The ruins of the Abbey and remnants of the foundations of its hospital
and chapel of St John that now lie beneath Hospitalfield House reflect the
widespread closure and destruction of monasteries throughout Scotland as a
result of the Reformation. This period saw the Hospitalfield estate pass from
Church to private ownership, eventually becoming the property of the Fraser
family in the mid-seventeenth century through James Fraser of Kirkton.[1] By
the nineteenth century, the estate's monastic connection was still remembered
and it was Hospitalfield's history that captured the imagination of Sir Walter
Scott. Hospitalfield and Arbroath served as inspiration for the estate of
Monksbarns and the town of Fairport, which form the setting for much of his
1816 novel *The Antiquary*. This connection not only increased the notoriety
of the Hospitalfield estate, but brought together the couple that irrevocably
changed the site's future.

One half of this couple was Patrick Allan, who was born in Arbroath to
Robert Allan and Isabel McDonald (sometimes appearing as Macdonald) in
1812. The Allans and the McDonalds were families of business owners and
skilled workers well known in Arbroath. Although Patrick's future in either his
paternal or maternal family businesses could have been assured, his passion for
art led him in a different direction. After completing his apprenticeship as a
decorative house painter in his uncle's firm, he was determined to continue his
education. This began at the Trustees' Academy in Edinburgh[2] under Sir William
Allan (not a relation of Patrick's). It continued as Patrick, alongside the painter
and future Director of the Trustees' Academy, Robert Scott Lauder, studied
great works of art and architecture in Rome and Paris. After his travels, Patrick
settled first in London and, afterwards, in Edinburgh, exhibiting with a group
of up-and-coming young painters known as 'the Clique' that included William
Powell Frith, Augustus Egg, Henry O'Neill, John Phillip, Edward Matthew
Ward and Thomas Brooks. In 1842, his commission from the Edinburgh
publishers Cadell to create illustrations for their new edition of *The Antiquary*
led him back to Arbroath.[3] In hindsight, Patrick's search at Hospitalfield for
source material for this commission seems fortuitous in the extreme, as there
he met his future wife, Elizabeth Fraser, the heiress to the Hospitalfield estate.

Elizabeth was the only daughter of Major John Fraser of Hospitalfield
and Elizabeth Parrott of Hawkesbury Hall, Warwickshire. As a young woman,
she was married to Lieutenant Arthur Baker of the 3rd Light Dragoons, but
was soon widowed. The circumstances that led this landed lady to marry an
aspiring artist has naturally led to many stories being conjured over the years.
Beyond these apocryphal tales, what is certain is that Patrick and Elizabeth
were married on 13 September 1843 and spent their lifetime together
supporting the development of art and artists.

Under Patrick's direction, Hospitalfield House was transformed. The Hospitalfield House that inspired Monksbarns was described by Scott in *The*

FIG. 1.1
The Picture Gallery, Hospitalfield

Antiquary as having: 'a solitary and sheltered appearance ... an irregular old-fashioned building, some part of which had belonged to a grange, or solitary farmhouse, inhabited by the bailiff, or steward, of the monastery, when the place was in possession of the monks'.[4] In the survey of Scottish buildings by John Gifford, however, Hospitalfield House is characterised as a 'Victorian red sandstone Scottish Baronial fantasy from which peeps out an earlier Laird's House'[5] which, interestingly, in its asymmetric floorplan and stylistic idiosyncrasies, resembled Scott's own home of Abbotsford. In one sense, Patrick's remodelling of Hospitalfield using the same iconic red of the twelfth-century Arbroath Abbey, and a façade that evoked the Scottish Baronial style of the sixteenth century, can be seen as contemporary with the Victorian trend toward architectural revivals. In another sense, aspects of this renovation were also part of a highly personal endeavour that reflected his passion for art in all its forms. As the artist George Hay later described, Hospitalfield House: 'bears in almost its every part and feature, externally and internally, the stamp of Mr. Allan-Fraser's mind and of his and his friends' experiences in art and in life.'[6] Integral to the extension of the original structure was a picture gallery to display his own work as well as sculpture, furniture and objects collected on his travels. Hung prominently on the walls of the galleries was work by 'the Clique' painters with whom he exhibited as a young artist, as well as paintings by contemporaries such as William Kidd, Robert Scott Lauder and Alexander Bell Middleton. Among these paintings is a group of specially commissioned self-portraits.

STORIES OF COURTSHIP

Patrick and Elizabeth's acquaintance and courtship has all the elements of a romance novel. A widow and heiress spending her days in the grandeur of a mansion house is charmed, falls in love and marries a dashing artist. It is, therefore, unsurprising that numerous variations of this story have developed through the years.

In the article 'Hospitalfield: "A Home of Ancient Peace"' that appeared in the November 1947 issue of The Scots Magazine, *James Rhynd relayed the following tale. The young Patrick went to Hospitalfield as a house painter and there met Elizabeth. She, impressed by his ambition, then supported his studies in Edinburgh and Rome. He subsequently returned to paint her portrait, and 'when he shows the finished work to her, the lady asks him which he prefers, the portrait or its original. He chooses the original and the lady and he are married.'[7] In his telling, Rhynd admitted it was 'a story which may be apocryphal ... if it be not true, we would like it to have been true.'[8]*

Rhynd's story has roots in earlier versions, which also hinge around the painting of a portrait. A.H. Millar, in his 1896 Art Journal *article, described how Elizabeth 'was married in 1843 to Patrick Allan, a young artist in Arbroath, who had been commissioned to paint the portraits of herself and her mother, and with whom she had fallen in love'.[9] The fanciful pen of the author of a 1902 article in* The Graphic *added further romance to this version by describing: 'When Patrick Allan — after a time at the Continental Schools — discovered his power of reproducing poetry on canvas, he was commissioned to paint a portrait of the fair owner of Hospitalfield — the daughter of Major Fraser; and she eventually became his wife.'[10] A triptych including portraits of Elizabeth and her mother painted by Patrick along with his self-portrait still hang in Hospitalfield House today. It is possible that this portrait of Elizabeth was the one that the authors attributed to the couple's blossoming love.*

In his 1990 Hospitalfield House, *William Payne suggested the possibility of a 'more realistic scenario'[11] for their marriage, in which Patrick's maternal uncle, involved in managing the Fraser estate, was instrumental in introducing his nephew to Elizabeth. Whatever brought them together, it seems their difference in social standing raised suspicion in Arbroath. As Alec Sturrock's article 'Patrick Allan-Fraser of Hospitalfield', from the March 1949 edition of* Scottish Field, *asserted: 'There seems to have been a certain amount of gossip in Arbroath ... Patrick Allan left town and spent the residue of his bachelordom at the Roxburghshire Manse of his cousin Rev. David Sturrock.'[12]*

Whether it was love at first sight or good feeling that grew over time, it seems Patrick and Elizabeth's marriage, as The Dundee Courier & Argus *described in 1890: 'was a happy one'.[13]*

The way in which Patrick remodelled Hospitalfield House also reflected his belief that the way to aid those of a lower socio-economic status was not through charity, but by helping individuals to obtain an education and livelihood — an idea that became widespread thanks to the work of political reformer and author Samuel Smiles. On this point, Patrick wrote in his 1861 manifesto on culture, society, economics and religion — titled *An Unpopular View of Our Times* — that: 'learning, like true religion, brings with it its own rewards and can only promote permanently the best interests of society.'[14] While never achieving the type of readership gained by Smiles' books, what Patrick painstakingly attempted to demonstrate through his rather lengthy prose, he did with ease through his actions. His support of local and early-stage artisans is evident in the many decoratively carved surfaces in each room of Hospitalfield House. The patterns in stone that lead up the main stairwell from the dark entryway to the sunlit, two-storey hall were crafted by Arbroath sculptor James Peters. His high-relief sculpture of a monk reading (fig. 1.2) that is positioned at the top of the first flight of stairs is a reminder of the site's monastic roots. Much of the carved design and patterning that adorn the picture gallery were the work of the young John Hutchison. After this early career opportunity, Hutchison went on to design and create sculptures for a variety of public places and historic sites throughout Scotland. It was another local craftsman, David Maver, who created the most intensively detailed wood carving at Hospitalfield (fig. 1.3). His delicately rendered representations of local flora made from fruitwood were installed as a multi-panelled ceiling, bringing a sense of nature into the interior.[15]

Like many educated and cultured Victorians, Patrick's interests were not confined by discipline. He engaged with art, politics, economics, religion, philosophy and science. He was a painter, designer, architect, collector, writer, civic leader and estate manager. Considering these many pursuits, it is unsurprising that disagreements have arisen in early twentieth-century and modern scholarship concerning whether Patrick's work as a painter, designer and architect were of true artistic merit or, instead, reflected the personal taste of an enthusiast.[16] Rather than trying to determine a value judgement, it is more constructive to view Patrick Allan-Fraser and his work as a product of a Victorian culture that encouraged curiosity and eclecticism. While Patrick was involved in a myriad of projects, what unified his multi-disciplinary approach was his desire to be a patron to those who had, or aspired to acquire, specialist skills and knowledge. It was for this reason that he was elected an Honorary Royal Scottish Academician in 1871.[17]

While Patrick was painting, orchestrating the House's remodelling and managing the estate, in what pursuits was Elizabeth engaged? Unfortunately,

FIG. 1.2

James Peters, High relief of a monk reading

image courtesy of Hospitalfield, 2017

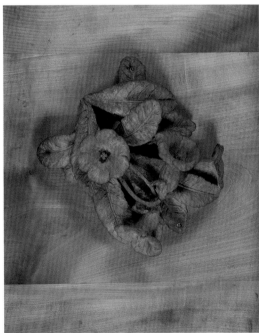

FIG. 1.3

David Maver, carved ceiling of the drawing room and panel detail

photographs © Ruth Clark, all rights reserved
images courtesy of Hospitalfield, 2017

little is known about Elizabeth's life before meeting Patrick and the absence of personal correspondence makes it difficult to surmise her personality, thoughts or opinions. The characterisation of Patrick and Elizabeth as a couple of 'kindred tastes' by *The Dundee Courier & Argus* suggests that she shared her husband's enthusiasm for art and approved of his changes to Hospitalfield House.[18] This is also indicated by Elizabeth's support for one of the stonemason's sons, James Dorward Lyall, later known as Durward Lely, to train as a tenor.[19] Although it is only through Patrick's eyes, more still can be interpreted about Elizabeth through his portrait of her (fig. 1.4). Depicted sitting by the fireplace at Hospitalfield House, Elizabeth embodies contentment and female virtue at its best. The sumptuous interior displays her wealth, while her simple clothing suggests humility. The fact that she appears to be thoughtfully reading conveys her education and desire for knowledge. In addition, the in-progress needlepoint in the background demonstrates her creativity and accomplishment. Within this context, the cat upon her lap can be seen as a symbol of peaceful, feminine domesticity as well as an indication of her love of animals.[20]

This portrait not only provides some insight into Elizabeth's character, as interpreted by Patrick, but also into their dynamic as a couple. By celebrating Elizabeth's virtues, it is clear that Patrick admired her. More can be inferred about their relationship from a triptych painted by Patrick, which today hangs in the Cedar Room, another addition to the house initiated by Patrick (fig. 1.5). In its left panel is Patrick, on the right is Elizabeth and in the centre is Elizabeth's mother, also called Elizabeth. By placing the elder Elizabeth in the middle, he showed respect for the family he married into. Portraying himself holding a brush and palette, he demonstrated his contribution to this lineage, his artistic flair. In depicting Elizabeth with her dog, Patrick once again shows her love of animals, and also her fidelity. His decision to merge the Fraser name with his own surname, Allan, upon coming into the legal inheritance of the estate when the elder Elizabeth died in 1851, publicly displayed his own fidelity and deference to the Fraser family.

If there was any doubt about the genuineness of Patrick and Elizabeth's relationship or his loyalty to her family, the Mortuary Chapel (fig. 1.6), designed by Patrick following his wife's death in 1873, sweeps this away. The Chapel resembles a miniature Hospitalfield House, with each corner sprouting a differently articulated turret. The relief-laden sandstone façade is matched by a highly decorative interior whose carved pattern of flora and fauna are referential to those at Hospitalfield House. By preparing himself a niche in order to be interred beside his late wife, within a building representative of their home and life together, Patrick was making a very public demonstration of his love for and devotion to Elizabeth.

If the Mortuary Chapel was a grand gesture, it was nothing in comparison with Patrick's plan for the future of Hospitalfield. As Patrick and Elizabeth had no children, there were no immediate heirs to their estate. Their legacy, like Hospitalfield House, would, instead, reflect their lifetime of cultivating art and artists. In 1873, Patrick drafted his *Deed of Settlement and Mortification*, which

A SUMMARY OF PATRICK ALLAN-FRASER'S BEQUEST

The primary aim of the bequest dedicated Allan-Fraser's land and capital to fund a school of art located at Hospitalfield House:

- *The art school would provide a four-year course of art education.*
- *Training would be given in painting, sculpture, woodcarving, architecture and engraving.*
- *Students would be young men between the ages of 16 and 18.*
- *Need for financial aid would be the primary consideration for admission.*
- *Students would reside at Hospitalfield House during their terms of study, receiving free room and board as well as a clothing allowance and medical treatment.*
- *Local people in Arbroath, male or female, interested in an art education would also be allowed to participate as non-residential day students.*
- *The Hospitalfield estate and the art school would be managed by appointed Trustees.*
- *The Trustees would select an established artist and qualified art teacher to act as 'Governor' to lead the students in their artistic, social and moral development.*
- *The Governor would preferably be married and would live at Hospitalfield with the students and his family. His wife would take on the role of 'Lady Supervisor', managing the day-to-day running of the house and its staff.*
- *A younger male artist, unmarried, would serve as the 'Assistant Governor' and would be responsible for the pastoral care of the students.*

The second objective, if the primary objective of founding an art school was achieved, was to host at Hospitalfield a maximum of four painters, three sculptors and three writers who were infirm or struggling financially.

The third objective, if sufficient funds remained, was to donate annually to the Artists' Benevolent Institution, London, for the education of orphan children as well as to Arbroath Town Council to continue Allan-Fraser's project of providing clean water to the town.[21]

FIG. 1.4
Patrick Allan-Fraser, Elizabeth Fraser

oil on canvas, 50 x 64 cm / Hospitalfield Collection, Arbroath / image courtesy of Hospitalfield, 2017

FIG. 1.5

The Cedar Room featuring a triptych by Patrick Allan-Fraser of himself, his mother-in-law Elizabeth Fraser, and his wife Elizabeth Fraser

began 'my Wife, Mrs. Elizabeth Allan-Fraser and I have long contemplated leaving part of our Means, Estate, and Effects for the advancement of Art'[22] and continued for many pages detailing a very specific plan for Hospitalfield to be transformed into a philanthropic centre for art and education.

This bequest can be interpreted as a response to several factors. Its detailed instructions were consistent with Patrick's fastidious nature, exemplified by the type of exacting control he exerted over the renovation of Hospitalfield House.[23] It can also be considered a gesture of empathy, as he knew from personal experience the type of training, encouragement and support aspiring artists in Scotland needed. While the school's socially conscious mission was consistent with Patrick and Elizabeth's pattern of patronage, it also aligned with the Victorian culture of philanthropy in which they lived. Two other Scottish art schools, whose legacies continue into the twenty-first century, were philanthropically founded at the end of the nineteenth and beginning of the twentieth century. Gray's School of Art in Aberdeen was established through the support of the industrialist John Gray in 1885.[24] The year 1909 saw the announcement of James Duncan of Jordanstone and Dumfork's bequest for the founding of an art school in Dundee. After many years of conflict and debate, his bequest ultimately supported the growth of art education in Dundee by supporting what is, today, the University of Dundee's Duncan of Jordanstone College of Art and Design.[25]

FIG. 1.6
The Mortuary Chapel, East View

Patrick and Elizabeth's bequest was a grand plan born out of their experiences and cultural milieu, embodying a spirit of creativity and optimism and ensuring that their legacy spanned beyond their lifetimes. Their vision was a captivating one. A few days after Patrick's death in 1890, headlines of this 'Remarkable Bequest' appeared in newspapers throughout Britain.[26] In the coming years, while the appointed Trustees prepared for the art school to open, this sense of anticipation and enthusiasm was continually rekindled. To this effect, A.H. Millar's 1896 *Art Journal* article 'Hospitalfield: A Proposed College for Artists' concluded that the art school: 'might have great influence in moulding the history of Scottish Art'.[27] Throughout the twentieth century, many changes would take place at Hospitalfield, causing its mission to diverge from that envisioned by Patrick and Elizabeth. Despite these changes, Hospitalfield would remain dedicated to the spirit of the bequest in its support of the development of artists and the art of Scotland.

2

From creation to collapse
The Allan-Fraser Art College
1890–1935

Patrick and Elizabeth's bequest had ambitious aims. Turning their vision into a reality proved a difficult task. It took the appointed Trustees[1] over ten years of planning and preparation to open the Allan-Fraser Art College[2] to its first students in 1902. The challenges, however, did not end once the College was established. Over the following 26 years, economic pressures would increasingly threaten the College's continuance until closure was the only option. Although the College was relatively short-lived, what it achieved from 1902 to 1928 was significant. Led by three successive artist-teachers, George Harcourt, RA, RP (1868–1947), Peter Munnoch (c.1870–1926) and Henry Daniel (1876–1959), it provided a unique form of art education to 75 students from five different countries. In doing so, it established an alternative model for learning at a time when art education was changing in Scotland. For the students, many of whom would not otherwise have been able to study art, it was the beginning of what would become their livelihood, and, for some, the start of careers that led to prominence.

Defining qualities of the Allan-Fraser Art College

Scottish Painting Past and Present: 1620–1908, published in 1908 and written by the artist, art critic and Director of the Scottish National Gallery, James L. Caw, was a significant art historical book of its era. That it highlighted the Allan-Fraser Art College implies that, within six short years, the College had established itself as a credible art education establishment. More than this, Caw's description provided insight into the qualities that distinguished the College from its contemporaries. When discussing education in Scotland, Caw wrote:

> Apart from the Central Art Schools there are, of course, in Edinburgh and Glasgow, private classes conducted by individual artists, and at Hospitalfield near Arbroath … there is an endowed school for painters … The Patrick Allan Fraser College of Art affords at present accommodation for some ten or a dozen students, who are taught and boarded free under the supervision of a resident master.[3]

One distinguishing aspect Caw observed of the College related to its funding. As it was supported by the Hospitalfield estate, it was an independent institution. This separated it from the Central Schools that were supported by and under the aegis of the Scottish Education Department (SED). As of 1908, these included Glasgow School of Art, Edinburgh College of Art and Gray's School of Art in Aberdeen. The College's independent status and source of funding allowed it to offer students an entirely free education. In contrast, the Central Schools could only offer a limited number of bursaries and scholarships.[4] Because of this, it was common practice that students who could not afford to study during the day would attend evening classes. These offerings paled in comparison to the free tuition, room and board provided by the Allan-Fraser Art College.

M.H. Spielmann, in his 1901 *The Magazine of Art* article, 'To Those Whom

FIG. 2.1
Isabella Scott Lauder, Priscilla the Puritan Maiden, *1862*

oil on canvas, 51 x 74 cm / Hospitalfield Collection, Arbroath / image courtesy of Hospitalfield, 2017

AUSTIN COOPER

The subsequent career of Austin Cooper (1890–1964) exemplifies the significance of the education the College provided. Born in Canada, Cooper moved with his family to Cardiff in 1896. After gaining preliminary training at the Cardiff School of Art, he was granted a scholarship to attend the College from 1906 until 1910. After serving in the Army during the First World War, he settled permanently in London, designing posters for London Northeast Railway and London Underground. It was for these iconic designs that he would be best known and from these experiences he wrote his 1938 instructional book, Making a Poster. *Later in life, Cooper returned to painting and developed a gestural abstract style, examples of which are in the Tate's collection.*[9]

It May Concern: The New Free Art University', predicted that the financial support the College provided its students would enable them to achieve: 'happy work and good living without anxiety'.[5] Indeed, the students at Hospitalfield valued these benefits. Former student Charles Robert Swift,[6] in his 1952 illustrated publication *Hospitalfield: The Home of the Antiquary*, reflected:

> It is a real joy to look back on those days of great happiness and impatiently vigorous imagination, lived amid delightful surroundings, where everything combined to develop ability and stimulate enthusiasm for hard work and application in preparation of one's career as an artist.[7]

Similarly, former student Austin Cooper, upon revisiting Hospitalfield in 1928:

> felt he owed everything to Hospitalfield ... apart from the value of the training, he and other old students he knows, felt the benefit of the life and influence at Hospitalfield and he contrasted it with the life of the student coming from the class from which he said he did, attending a school of art in any of the large centres.[8]

Students of the Allan-Fraser Art College lived and worked at Hospitalfield during their terms of study. This intensified the learning environment by allowing education to extend beyond the classroom to mealtimes and evenings; as the 1906 annual report to the Trustees revealed:

> There is much earnestness and enthusiasm for work amongst the students and this is to no small extent due to the Collegiate life at Hospitalfield, to the evenings spent together when Art subjects are discussed, when students share their sketches and original ideas.[10]

Although a lot of serious study took place at the College, the residential atmosphere also created a lively social community and bonds of friendship formed among the small group of students. For example, the 1905 report to the Trustees ended by stating: 'The Arbroath Hockey Club owes no small part of its success to the excellent help of the Hospitalfield players.'[11] In 1909, *The Scotsman* reported that students performed their collectively written melodrama *Gladys' Revenge* to an audience of eighty guests at Hospitalfield.[12] Many years later, when Frank Dobson, one of the students who took part in this play, recorded his recollections of the College, he included stories of late-night adventures from which he and his friends returned by shimmying up the drainpipes.[13] While this type of fun was usually harmless, the expulsion of Dobson's friend Bernard Adams also suggests that, occasionally, these antics breached the College's expectation of discipline.

Another feature of the College that distinguished it from its contemporaries was its differing enrolment policy regarding male and female students. Aspiring female artists were only permitted to enrol as day students, while male students were granted the full benefit of room and board as well as the advantages of the more informal after-hours teaching, which could occur during mealtime and evening discussions. It was not the principle of educating women in art to which Patrick Allan-Fraser objected. Within his collection there were several paintings by female artists, including *Priscilla the Puritan Maiden* by Isabella Scott Lauder (1808–1869) (fig. 2.1). Isabella was the daughter of the well-known Victorian painter, Robert Scott Lauder, who had been Patrick's friend as well as his former teacher at the Trustees' Academy.

Although her father's connections surely assisted Isabella in her career, her success was ultimately due to her own perseverance. As a founder member of the Edinburgh Ladies' Art Club and one of the first female students to study at the Trustees' Academy, Isabella was among a generation of female artists working to expand their educational and exhibition opportunities.[14]

Despite these opportunities, Victorian morality and differing societal expectations for men and women meant that the genders were still restricted to separate social and professional spheres. Allowing young unmarried male and female students to live within one house would have been considered morally and socially unacceptable during Patrick's lifetime, and that would still have been the case when the Trustees opened the College in 1902.[15] This is why Patrick's bequest detailed that only men could be residential students, but both men and women from Arbroath could participate as day students.[16]

By not offering equal places to men and women, the College was less progressive in regards to women's education than the coeducational non-residential art colleges in Aberdeen, Dundee, Edinburgh and Glasgow. Given the continued existence of gender inequality, its rules were by no means archaic. For example, the Royal Scottish Academy of Art and Architecture declared Frances McIan the first female Honorary Member in 1854, but did not allow women to become full members until 1944, when sculptor Phyllis Bone was elected.[17] Life-drawing classes were also commonly gender segregated and, in many cases, women were forbidden to work from a nude model.[18]

A 1904 annual report to the Trustees that described the arrangements for accommodating female life models illustrates the lengths to which the College went to ensure that the student body maintained proper social and moral decorum: 'Whilst employed at the college the models are suitably lodged & their comforts cared for by the wife of the keeper of the North Lodge – the models attending at the studios daily during working hours.'[19] This passage emphasises the distinct delineations between the professional and residential spheres of the female models and the male students. The report also relayed how the life models employed by the College were 'some of the best female models in London', a point which asserted their professionalism and made it clear that the students could not have future contact with them. This situation differed from the employment of the male models, 'found in the neighbourhood', whom the students may have, afterwards, seen locally.[20] These policies were consistent with those of other life classes in Scotland, such as those at the Royal Scottish Academy Life School, where: 'certain proprieties were maintained ... the models were provided with a changing room and the students were instructed never to point them out on the street.'[21]

There is no evidence to suggest that female day students from Arbroath ever studied at the College. The College did, however, experience the effects of the era's increasing rights for women. A 1914 article in *The Observer* declared that Hospitalfield's galleries, usually open to the public during the summer, would be closed due to 'numerous acts of malicious mischief now being perpetrated in the destruction of works of art in public galleries'.[22] The destruction the Trustees feared was not due to random acts of vandalism, but the campaigning of the suffragettes. Earlier in the year, the College's Governor, Peter Munnoch, was one of several visitors to the Royal Scottish Academy who witnessed a suffragette take an axe to John Lavery's portrait of King George.[23] If such an attack could occur in the galleries of the Academy, it is unsurprising that Munnoch would have viewed Hospitalfield's galleries as being vulnerable. The two sculptures of female nudes would have been of particular concern, as such sculptures, along with portraits of political figures, were often targets.

FRANK DOBSON AND BERNARD ADAMS

From the accounts of Frank Dobson, RA, CBE (1886–1963), Bernard Adams, RP, ROI, NS (1884–1965), on returning to his home in London after his expulsion from the Allan-Fraser Art College, regretted his youthful indiscretions. Recommitting himself to studying art, he attended the Westminster School of Art and Antwerp Academy. Adams became particularly known for his portraits and landscapes and was elected to the Royal Society of Portrait Painters, Royal Society of Oil Painters, and National Society of Painters, Sculptors and Engravers.

Dobson completed his course of study at the College and reunited with Adams in London in 1910. Knowing his former classmate was without money or resources, Adams offered Dobson a place to stay until he could establish himself. Although Dobson had experimented with clay modelling during his time at the College, his focus had been on painting, and it was not until the 1920s that he discovered his true affinity for the medium of sculpture. He soon became one of Britain's premier Modernist sculptors, exhibiting alongside Henry Moore and Barbara Hepworth, and served as Professor of Sculpture at the Royal College of Art from 1946 to 1953. For his artistic innovations, he was elected to the Royal Academy and awarded a CBE.[24]

THE 'UNOFFICIAL' FEMALE STUDENTS OF HOSPITALFIELD

While there were no female students admitted fully to the College, it seems artistic tutelage went on within the family of the first Governor, George Harcourt. His wife, Mrs Mary Lascelles Harcourt (née Leesmith), was a practising artist who exhibited at the Royal Academy from 1892 until 1922. Although there is no evidence to suggest she undertook any formal teaching responsibilities at the College, it is likely both she and her husband instructed their daughters Anne, Elizabeth Aletha and Mary Edeva, all of whom exhibited work at the Royal Academy later in life.

A stark contrast is found between George Harcourt's depictions of his daughters. His 1921 portrait of (Dorothy) Anne is a sumptuous painting that conveys feminine sophistication, humility and grace, while his 1942 painting of Elizabeth Aletha captures a heroic, confident and assertive woman in an ambulance driver's uniform. Perhaps these differences reveal something of the varying character of his daughters, yet it is also possible that they simply reflect changes brought about in twentieth-century British society – changes which would, eventually, also be reflected at Hospitalfield.[25]

Residential life at the College also meant that the students, unlike their contemporaries studying in Aberdeen, Edinburgh and Glasgow, lived and worked in a stately home in the countryside outside the town of Arbroath, rather than in the midst of an industrial city. To ensure that the students were connected to the art of Scotland's urban centres, annual trips to see exhibitions in Edinburgh and Glasgow were arranged.[26]

The College's countryside setting otherwise proved a visual asset that presented an opportunity for landscape and animal painting, which the art colleges in urban locations could not offer. There were precedents in Scotland for training students in landscape and animal painting within a country setting. *En plein air* painting was a central practice of artists of the late nineteenth century who settled in rural artist colonies across Europe and the United Kingdom. It was within this climate of interest in immersion in the pastoral landscape that Joseph Denovan Adam established his Country Atelier (1887–1895) outside Stirling for: 'Artists and Art Students ... for the study of animals ... observing animal life in its usual surroundings and also in its relation to landscape of varied character'.[27]

That the College engaged with this tradition is exemplified by the 1903 annual report, which recorded:

> They have the exceptional opportunity of studying animal life at the House Farm which is so conveniently situated [near] to the College. This is specially taken advantage of by one of the students who has a particular gift for animal painting.[28]

The student mentioned could be none other than the young John Murray Thomson, RSA, RSW (1885–1974). After attending the College from 1902 to 1906, Thomson enjoyed a successful career as an animal painter in Edinburgh that saw him elected to the Royal Scottish Academy of Art and Architecture and Royal Scottish Society of Painters in Watercolours.[29] His animal paintings not only reveal his understanding of anatomy, but convey a sense of the animals' movements and characters, ennobling the often seemingly humble subjects. Furthermore, his passion for his subject matter is evident in *Animals We Know*, a book of facts and stories which he co-authored and illustrated in 1924. No doubt it was the practice of observation from life, which he began at the College, that enabled him to create such animated images.

The final characteristic that distinguished the Allan-Fraser Art College can be found by returning to Caw's description, which began with the phrase: 'apart from the Central Art Schools'.[30] Unlike Glasgow School of Art, Edinburgh College of Art and Gray's School of Art in Aberdeen, the College was independent from the SED. The SED-approved curricula, which the three Central Schools taught as of 1909, evolved in parallel with Allan-Fraser Art College, with Glasgow School of Art being the first to institute its new curriculum in 1901.[31] Prior to this, the dominant method of art education in Scotland and throughout the United Kingdom was the South Kensington System – a highly structured, multi-staged curriculum which became a fiercely contested issue as the nineteenth century progressed. During this period, there were many small independent schools and classes running outside the South Kensington System.

Within this educational climate, it was common for students' studies to extend for varying lengths of time and for students to study at a variety of institutions. This pattern continued into the early twentieth century. Many of the College's students began their studies elsewhere before they attended and continued their education at other schools following their four years at the College. Once the SED began to regulate Scotland's art education, however,

FIG. 2.2

Unknown, Standing Nude with a Paintbrush, c.*1910*

oil on canvas, 92 x 51 cm / Hospitalfield Collection, Arbroath / image courtesy of Hospitalfield, 2017

THE ALLAN-FRASER
ART COLLEGE'S FIRST TERM

The first term at the College, for the students, their Governor and the Trustees was in many ways an experiment that presented unforeseen challenges. While the idea of student life in a stately home may have seemed idyllic, Hospitalfield House proved inhospitable accommodation. According to the Governor's 1902 report to the Trustees:

'During the influenza students were considerably interrupted in their work ... Hospitalfield is a very difficult house to heat in cold weather, especially on the ground floor where the student bedrooms are ... As things stand at present the long stone corridors and stairs which have to be washed and the carrying of coal in a house as inconvenient for servant's work as Hospitalfield make servants afraid of the work in the winter and some of them have left in consequence.'[32]

Luckily, the Trustees heeded these words and the living conditions were remedied before the following winter.

the qualifications they granted to students became the established standard. This streamlined the way students studied art and caused the number of outlying institutions to dwindle.

Within this transitional period at the beginning of the twentieth century, the College presented an alternative educational model that harkened back to the centuries-old master-apprentice tradition. At the College, a head teacher, known as the Governor, taught a small group of students. This learning dynamic reflected what Patrick Allan-Fraser had experienced at the Trustees' Academy and differed from the broader faculty base and larger student numbers of the Central Schools. Although the College's educational model looked more towards the past than the future, its variance from what was becoming the new mainstream trend in education indicated that the debate about how to best educate an artist would be ongoing.

While the College's distinguishing qualities continuously shaped the educational experience, this was also influenced by the particular outlook and practice of the Governor. As the Governor controlled every aspect of teaching, he exerted great influence over the curriculum and the students. The character of the education the College provided as well as the development of the students was, therefore, impacted by the individual ethos of each successive Governor.

A BRIEF TIMELINE OF ART EDUCATION IN SCOTLAND

1729: The Academy of St Luke, the first known educational group for artists, is founded in Edinburgh. It runs for only two years.

1753: Robert and Andrew Foulis establish the Foulis Academy in Glasgow. Financial difficulties cause it to close in 1776.

1760: The Board of Trustees for the Encouragement of Manufacturers in Scotland open an art school in Edinburgh known as the Trustees' Academy.

1853: The South Kensington System is instituted at the seventeen Central Schools for Art established throughout the UK by the Department of Science and Art.

1872: The Scottish Educational Department (SED) secedes from the Department of Science and Art, but the South Kensington System remains the predominant method of teaching.

1892: Architect Robert Rowand Anderson founds a School for Applied Art in Edinburgh in opposition to the South Kensington System.

1901: The Allan-Fraser Art College appoints its first Governor and prepares to accept applicants. Glasgow School of Art is the first Central School to introduce a new SED-approved curriculum.

1902: The first eight art students arrive at the Allan-Fraser Art College.

1904: A new SED-approved curriculum is introduced at Gray's School of Art.

1909: A new SED-approved curriculum is introduced at Edinburgh College of Art, which merged the Trustees' Academy and the Royal Scottish Academy Life School.

1929: Dundee Technical College and School of Art becomes the fourth Central School with an SED-approved drawing and painting curriculum.

1962: Dundee's college of art is officially renamed Duncan of Jordanstone College of Art and Design.

1992: Gray's School of Art becomes part of the newly formed Robert Gordon University.

1994: Duncan of Jordanstone College of Art and Design joins the University of Dundee.

2011: Edinburgh College of Art joins the University of Edinburgh.[33]

George Harcourt, Governor 1901–9

By the time George Harcourt was appointed as Governor in 1901, he had already established a significant reputation as a talented British painter. Since 1893, his work had been exhibited annually at the Royal Academy and he had featured in exhibitions in Paris. Whether interpreting literary narratives or composing genre scenes, Harcourt became known for his delicate treatment of light and texture and his ability to imbue the figures involved in these tableaux with life and character.[34] This is exemplified by his 1910 *The Birthday* (fig. 2.4). In *The Birthday*, Harcourt depicted his wife surrounded by their children in a richly decorated interior. Although dated the year following his departure from the College, there is little doubt that it was begun earlier, as the tapestry in the background can still be seen hanging in Hospitalfield House today (fig. 2.3). Through his soft, but detailed, rendering of the tapestry, the rug and the ladies' dresses, Harcourt added layers of pattern and texture to the image that combined to create a sumptuous, luxurious atmosphere. His treatment of the natural light dappling across the tapestry and illuminating the faces of the seated figures reaffirmed this sense of delicacy. The elegant setting also complements the femininity of his wife, Mary, whose dress and shawl cascade around her. Mary, however, is more than just a beautiful model. She is shown focusing intently on her reading, and the fact that this is emulated by her youngest daughter, Dorothy, proves that Mary's behaviour sets a good example for her children. With Mary acting as a role model for Dorothy, and her son, George, looking to her with interest and attention, this image borders on the idealised,

FIG. 2.3

The Drawing Room, Hospitalfield, featuring the tapestry in George Harcourt's The Birthday

photograph © Ruth Clark / image courtesy of Hospitalfield, 2017

FIG. 2.4

George Harcourt, The Birthday, *1910*

oil on canvas, 180.5 x 267 cm / Lady Lever Art Gallery, Port Sunlight Village, Wirral, transferred from Lord Leverhulme's private collection, 1922
image courtesy of National Museums Liverpool, 2017

FIG. 2.5
Allan Newton Sutherland,
Portrait of a Bearded Man

oil on canvas, 91.8 x 70.1 cm / Aberdeen Art Gallery & Museums Collections,
Aberdeen (transferred in 1999 from the Central Library) / image courtesy
of Aberdeen Art Gallery & Museums, 2017

and perhaps slightly sentimental, school of family portraiture. Yet the way in which Harcourt captured the character of his other daughters prevented it from becoming saccharine. His middle daughter, Elizabeth Aletha, looks at her mother with an impatient intensity and precocious quality, adding a certain authenticity to the family dynamic. Furthermore, the captivating outward gaze of the eldest daughter, Mary Edeva, both invites the viewer to engage with the image and also conveys this young adolescent's strength of character. With this display of technical skill and emotional engagement, it is little wonder that *The Birthday* won a gold medal at the Amsterdam International Exhibition of 1912.

Comparing a figure study[35] that John A.M. Hay, RP (1887–1960), painted during his time at the College between 1906 and 1910 with a description of Harcourt's process of painting reveals how skills regarding representing the human form were transferred from teacher to student. Frederic Lees, in his 1917 *The Studio* article 'The Art of George Harcourt', summarised Harcourt's method of life painting: 'After preparing a slight sketch of the composition and colour, he designs the picture direct on the canvas, evolving his ideas as he proceeds.'[36] In Hay's figure study, the face and the hand clasping the book have the greatest tonal range and have been treated with the most sensitivity. The contrast between these developed areas and the basic rendering of the drapery and the broad strokes of the background are evidence that he was applying Harcourt's process of evolving the painting directly on the canvas.[37] This spontaneous process of developing images distinguished teaching under Harcourt from that at the Central Schools, where pupils made a final painting only after its composition was determined using a series of preparatory studies.[38] For Hay, this foundational training proved particularly significant as he subsequently became a successful portrait painter in Chelsea.[39]

Many of the techniques in portraiture that Harcourt passed on to the students at the College can be attributed to his own training with the artist Hubert von Herkomer (1849–1914). Herkomer was a financially and critically successful Victorian artist. Although he made his reputation with paintings of the poverty and difficulty of rural life, he was also a highly sought after and accomplished portraitist. As a student, he, like many others of his contemporaries, found the South Kensington System too rigid in its curriculum and too heavily focused on learning to draw from the antique. The art school he established at Bushey in Hertfordshire, which ran from 1883 to 1904, therefore sought to remedy the aspects of the South Kensington system with which he disagreed. Herkomer encouraged students to develop and study in a way more tailored to their talents and allowed them to work from the life model and from nature at an early stage in their training. Like the College, Herkomer's school was a small-scale, independent, country-based art institution run in the master-apprentice tradition. As a young artist, Harcourt flourished under Herkomer's direction and progressed to the level of Assistant Professor. When Harcourt became Governor at Hospitalfield, with the freedom to establish his own regime, in many ways he recreated Herkomer's system of education.[40]

In a lecture at the Royal Academy, Herkomer proclaimed that: 'truly an art that can bring a living individual before our eyes is a great art.'[41] The way Herkomer and Harcourt captured both the features and personalities of their sitters suggests that their paintings could be classed, according to Herkomer's own standard, as great art. The legacy at the College of capturing the character of the sitter through colour, composition and form becomes evident through comparing paintings by Harcourt with the subsequent work of his students.

Harcourt's *Arbroath Whist Club* (fig. 2.6) presents a group portrait that emphasises the features and dispositions of each individual. For example, the rightmost figure in the foreground turns to the viewer with judgement

FIG. 2.6

George Harcourt, Arbroath Whist Club, *1914*

oil on canvas, 204 x 304 cm / Angus Council Collections managed by ANGUSalive Museums, Galleries & Archives (transferred from Arbroath Town Council) / image courtesy of Angus Council, 2017

in his narrowed eyes, while the man to his right (viewer's left) stands proudly with his shoulders back and gaze fixed on the distance. When the figures in this painting are compared with *Portrait of a Bearded Man* (fig. 2.5) by Allan Newton Sutherland (*c.*1885–1918)[42] there can be no question that Sutherland was a student of Harcourt. Not only did Sutherland similarly allow a sense of pure light to illuminate the features of his sitter, but he gave the subject's thoughtful, but endlessly captivating, gaze the type of intensity and individual character of the figures in *Arbroath Whist Club*.

Comparing Harcourt's handling in *The Birthday* with subsequent work by students Thomas Percival Anderson (1885–1940)[43] and Arnold Mason, RA, RP (1885–1963),[44] provides further evidence of Harcourt's influence. Anderson's painting of Edith Anderson (fig. 2.9) displays a similar delicacy and detailing in his treatment of his sitter's clothing. This, as in Harcourt's group portrait, heightens the grace and femininity of his subject's bearing. These qualities are also evident in Mason's portrait of Olive Mary Wolryche-Whitmore (fig. 2.7). Although Mason's early portraits show a Harcourt-like reliance on creating drama through the contrast of light and dark, in his portrait of Wolryche-Whitmore, his palette lightens, allowing the features and clothes of the sitter to connect with her surroundings to create visual cohesion. In this way, Mason's portrait of Wolryche-Whitmore marks a transitional point in Mason's style, which, in its mature phase, would be characterised by a bolder use of colour and more painterly brushwork.

While Harcourt, like Herkomer, used his own methods and aesthetics as models for his students to follow, neither were dogmatic teachers. Herkomer believed that art education should be adapted to the student. Part of this personalisation involved establishing an understanding between student and teacher. To this extent he wrote:

> The longer my experience the more certain I am that the art faculty in every human being is worked by his character ... How often have I found that a careful search into the character of the student has helped me to understand the cause of certain blunders in his art studies.[45]

This philosophy was echoed in Harcourt's 1905 report to the Trustees, which stated that the College provided

> ... the opportunity of better knowing the student individually and of studying his temperament and idiosyncrasies. Often some difficulty in regard to the student's work may be overcome by attending to some tendency in his character.[46]

By getting to know the students' personalities as well as their artistic abilities Harcourt, like Herkomer, guided them in the investigation of artistic media and genres to which they were most suited.

The result of the personalised education that Harcourt provided can be seen in the diversity of the careers and later artwork of his students. John Thomson's animal paintings, Charles Robert Swift's book illustrations and Austin Cooper's poster designs, which have already been mentioned, provide some examples as to the way Harcourt's tutelage allowed his students to gain different skill-sets that, in turn, allowed them to pursue different career paths. There are differences, too, in the actual style of painting among ex-students. After studying under Harcourt, Robert Timmis (1886–1960) continued to paint while teaching at Liverpool Art School, while James Bell Anderson

FIG. 2.8

James Bell Anderson, Still Life, *c.1932–3*

oil on canvas, 50.8 x 60.9 cm / Glasgow Museums and Libraries Collections, Glasgow (purchased 1933)
image © CSG CIC Glasgow Museums and Libraries Collections

FIG. 2.9
Thomas Percival Anderson, Mrs. Edith Anderson, *1907*

oil on canvas, 115 x 87 cm / York Museum Trust, York (gift from R.W. Anderson, 1946) / image courtesy of York Museum Trust, 2017

(1886–1938) became an established portrait painter in Glasgow and a member of the Royal Scottish Academy of Art and Architecture.[47] Anderson's *Still Life* (fig. 2.8) has a crisp clarity that demonstrates his ability to paint with convincing realism. This is particularly effective in his representation of the smooth reflective surfaces of the ceramics, contrasted with the softer organic textures of fruit. This careful rendering of light upon the still-life, and detailed treatment of the objects' reflection, imbues the picture with a sense of stillness. Anderson's aesthetic differed greatly from that of Timmis, whose painterly approach celebrated colour and pattern. Using loose brushstrokes, Timmis emphasised the movement of light across highly patterned tapestries and vases, thereby creating dynamic layers of visual interest.

Harcourt taught his students to paint as he painted, as a master would teach his apprentices. Those students, like Sutherland or Hay, who became portrait painters owed much of their technique to their training at the College. As Harcourt's approach was tempered by applying Herkomer's philosophy of encouraging students to develop their individual talents, his students also became artists in their own right, rather than straightforward disciples. This meant that those students with different affinities benefited from an environment within which they could be cultivated.

After seven years of teaching at the College, Harcourt returned to England. There he continued to exhibit his work and was elected an associate member of the Royal Academy in 1919, becoming a full member in 1926.[48] The precedent he established at the College, however, would be modified as the new Governor's regime reflected a different point of reference and approach to art and education.

Peter Munnoch, Governor 1909–26

In 1909, Peter Munnoch was appointed George Harcourt's successor. Although he was a less established painter than Harcourt had been when he became Governor, Munnoch had been one of the Royal Scottish Academy Life School's most promising young pupils, winning travelling scholarships and awards.[49] Past employers also recommended his artistic and teaching abilities very highly: 'I have much pleasure in bearing testimony of my high appreciation of Mr. Munnoch as a student under my supervision. He possesses good art ability, being also thoroughly conscientious and painstaking in all he undertakes';[50] and 'All the work entrusted to him he arranged and carried out systematically and with the best results; proved himself to be a careful, painstaking, reliable and efficient teacher.'[51]

Few examples of Munnoch's work remain and, unlike Harcourt, he did not continue to exhibit or take commissions during his time as Governor. It seems that, for Munnoch, teaching art was his true passion and primary priority. To this effect, he wrote in his 1924 Report to the Trustees: 'Being devoted to Art and greatly interested in Art Education ... I have always devoted more time to it than was in my bond. I found my work in the development of the abilities of the young artists.'[52] At the College, Munnoch proved a devoted teacher who combined two seemingly disparate approaches: the discipline of traditional art educational methods and experimental work with contemporary aesthetics.

Munnoch's painting of *Mrs Anne Bruce of Arnot* (fig. 2.10),[53] after the original by eighteenth-century Scottish painter Allan Ramsay, is evidence that, as a student, he learned representational values by looking to the art of the past. Photographs that show students standing next to their paintings of plaster casts and Munnoch's request for the Trustees to purchase art history books indicate that, based on his training, he encouraged students to learn from the Old Masters.[54] Drawing from casts of Classical sculptures and

FIG. 2.10

Peter Munnoch (after Allan Ramsay), Mrs Anne Bruce of Arnot

oil on canvas, 75 x 62.7 cm / Angus Council Collections managed by ANGUSalive Museums, Galleries & Archives (gift from Mrs. Munnoch, 1934)
image courtesy of Angus Council, 2017

JOHN BULLOCH SOUTER

*John Bulloch Souter (1890–1972) began his art
education at Gray's School of Art in 1907, attended
the Allan-Fraser Art College from 1909 to 1913
and, afterwards, returned to Gray's School of Art,
achieving a travelling scholarship to Europe.
Moving to London in 1922, he became a well-
known portrait painter and regular exhibitor at the
Royal Academy. His most controversial painting,*
The Breakdown, *created a scandal in London
when it was exhibited at the Royal Academy in
1926. Although lauded by art critics, its depiction
of a nude white female dancing to music played
by a black saxophonist was considered potentially
inflammatory by the Colonial Secretary, who
ordered that it be removed from the walls of the
Academy. Devastated, Souter painted over the
monumental canvas. It was only once he returned
to Aberdeen that he repainted a smaller version
of* The Breakdown *in 1962. Today, the breadth
of work Souter produced is represented in the
Aberdeen Art Gallery and Museum's collection.*[55]

copying Old Master works were educational exercises that had been practised
by young painters in Scotland since the eighteenth century and persisted in
most art schools in the United Kingdom into the twentieth century. While
Harcourt's emphasis on students working from the live model allied the
College with Herkomer's approach, Munnoch's methods connected it with
the curricula taught in Aberdeen, Dundee, Edinburgh and Glasgow.

The *c.*1909 painting (fig. 2.12) by student John Bulloch Souter (see left),
after Titian's *c.*1510 *Portrait of a Man in a Red Cap*,[56] exemplifies how Munnoch's students learned painting techniques by copying great works of art.
While the deterioration of the painting's surface makes it difficult to assess
whether Souter achieved Titian's luminous tones, his ability to adopt Titian's
composition and delicate rendering of textures makes his painting a successful
student copy. While Munnoch valued the art of the past, he also had a taste
for the contemporary and encouraged his students to cultivate an interest in
modern painting. It was this type of formative influence that surely contributed
to the innovative, and at times controversial, work Souter produced later in his
career.

The students' introduction to contemporary art via Munnoch was also
evident during the College's annual excursions to Edinburgh and Glasgow.
On these occasions, he encouraged students to see exhibitions of French
Impressionism and visit Miss Cranston's Willow Tea Rooms, whose interior
and furniture had been recently designed by Charles Rennie Mackintosh
(1868–1928) in 1903. Students also experimented with modern aesthetics at
the College. A *c.*1920 photograph from Hospitalfield's archives which features
an unidentified student's landscape painting is evidence of the student's use
of loose brushwork to convey the effect of the changing light. This stylistic

FIG. 2.11
Stanley Horace Gardiner, Castallack, Lamorna Valley

oil on board, 58.5 x 67 cm / private collection, on loan to Penlee House Gallery & Museum, Penzance
© the artist's estate, all rights reserved / image courtesy of Penlee House & Museum, 2017

FIG. 2.12

John Bulloch Souter (after Titian), Portrait of a Man in a Red Cap

oil on canvas, 90.5 x 69 cm / Hospitalfield Collection, Arbroath / © the artist's estate, all rights reserved / image courtesy of Hospitalfield, 2017

approach recalled that of the French Impressionists. Similar aesthetic qualities are also evident in the later work of Stanley Horace Gardiner (1888–1952), who was a student of the College from 1910 to 1914. Settling in the Lamorna valley of Cornwall, Gardiner frequently painted landscapes in an Impressionist style.[57] In his *Castallack, Lamorna Valley* (fig. 2.11), Gardiner employed freely and thickly applied paint to capture a sense of the fleeting light moving across the landscape, whose warmth he conveyed through the reappearance of orange highlights.

While Munnoch directed students to study both old and new artistic references in order to apply them to their work, he, like Harcourt, also encouraged them to discover their own artistic affinities. For student Frank Dobson, this freedom of experimentation meant that his time at the College was

> ... the most formative experience of my life ... I tried all sorts of methods of drawing, particularly the pen and ink sketches by Rembrandt, also the drawings in red chalk by Watteau, Fragonard and, later, Alfred Steven, after a time I began to discover a style of my own.[58]

The critical success that many of Munnoch's students attained in a wide variety of styles and genres suggests that the formative impact his teaching had on Dobson also affected others. For example, the education at the College prepared Adam Sherriff Scott (1887–1980) for a diverse and adventurous career. Soon after finishing his studies he emigrated to Canada and there designed posters for the Canadian Pacific Railway, undertook private commissions for paintings of the Western landscape, lived with and painted Inuit communities, and was eventually elected as a full member of the Royal Canadian Academy of Art in 1942.[59]

Hospitalfield and the First World War

The First World War caused dramatic changes for the College. With an all-male student body, enlistment rapidly decreased their numbers. By the first term of 1915, only two students were resident at Hospitalfield. Throughout the following years, enrolment fluctuated as students left for and returned from service. Out of the seventeen students enrolled at the College between 1914 and 1918, nine are known to have served in the armed forces with two additional students leaving for unspecified, but likely war-related, reasons.

Also among those to fight in the First World War were many former students of the College.

One of these was Canadian-born Kenneth Forbes, OSA, RCA (1892–1980), who was wounded and gassed during his service with the Royal Fusiliers. After recovering from his injuries, he was reassigned to the Machine Gun Corps before eventually becoming one of Canada's War Artists. Forbes's paintings present unrelenting images of war.[60] His painting *Canadian Artillery in Action* (fig. 2.13) depicts the Canadian gunners' support of the British troops on 16 July 1916 during the Battle of the Somme. Capturing the heat of battle, Forbes conveys both the strength and exhaustion of the soldiers, as the muscular forms of the foreground figures are contrasted with the slumped figures in the background. Through the crumbling landscape, the explosion from the canon, and the atmospheric sky, this image emphasises the brutal, all-encompassing sensory experience of war.

Of the current and former College students to fight, Thomas McGregor Douglas, Adam George Galloway, Brian Hatton, Allan Newton Sutherland, Albert John Warr and Hubert Thomas Ward are known to have been killed in action.[61] In 1915, Munnoch also suffered the additional loss of his brother and fellow artist John Munnoch (see overleaf).

FIG. 2.13

Kenneth Keith Forbes, Canadian Artillery in Action, *1918*

oil on canvas, 157.5 x 245.3 cm / Canadian War Museum, Ottawa, Canada / image courtesy of Bridgeman Images, 2017

ARTISTS AND BROTHERS:
PETER AND JOHN MUNNOCH

Among their eleven siblings, Peter and John shared a special bond and a passion for art. Although Peter was several years younger, it seems John began his artistic training later in life. By the time Peter became Governor of the College, John was just beginning his training at Edinburgh College of Art. Several landscapes of Arbroath (fig. 2.14) and a portrait of Peter, painted by John c.1910, suggest that John spent time at Hospitalfield. The vibrant colours and painterly handling of these works reveal that John, like his brother Peter, was interested in Impressionism.

When the First World War began, John was on a sketching holiday in the Netherlands. Shortly after his prompt return to Scotland, he joined the 5th Battalion of the Royal Scots in 1915. He served with his Battalion for only three months before being killed in action. The significance of the relationship between Peter and John is captured in the will John wrote before he went to war in which he specified: 'Of the goods I possess I wish my brother Peter to take all, in return for his great goodness to me.'[62] Peter kept his brother's paintings for the rest of his life and it is thanks to the donation of Peter's wife Jane, who survived him, that several of John's works are now in the collections of Angus Council and the Stirling Smith Art Gallery.[63]

FIG. 2.14
John Munnoch, Hospitalfield
oil on board, 35.3 x 25.2 cm / Hospitalfield Collection, Arbroath / image courtesy of Hospitalfield, 2017

Munnoch's aptitude for teaching and genuine concern for his students made him a particularly adept artistic and pastoral leader during this period. This is reflected in the sensitivity with which he wrote his 1915 report to the Trustees:

> Owing to the small number of students and the general uncertainty prevailing, it was not expedient to carry on the programme of work quite as systematically as in former years ... The average quality of the actual work done has not been up to that of previous years, but when allowance is made for the prevailing unrest that is not without its effect in the College...on the whole they have worked well and made good progress.[64]

As Munnoch's report reveals, during the war years, the teaching schedule was adjusted, made more flexible to accommodate the College's changing and uncertain population of students. The balance of the curriculum was also readjusted. Owing to the College's diminishing finances and the increased difficulty of securing models, there was less figure drawing and a greater emphasis on painting and drawing the landscape.[65] One wonders if this emphasis was also motivated by the rationale that time spent in the quietness of nature would benefit those students returning from the horrors of war. For those students who could not enlist or were discharged because of medical conditions, it can be surmised that Hospitalfield offered a safe haven from the social stigma attached to young men who could not serve. Unfortunately, there are no surviving examples of student work from this period, which could have provided additional insight into if or how the students' experiences of war impacted their choice of imagery or aesthetic.

Wartime also brought financial hardship upon the Hospitalfield estate, which continued to suffer throughout the recession that followed. This caused the Trustees to become increasingly uncertain about the future of the College. In the midst of this fiscal turmoil, Munnoch's unexpected death from a sudden heart attack in 1926 was an additional shock. Over his seventeen years at the College, he established a system of education that enabled students to learn from Old and Modern Masters alike. His synthesis of influences meant his teaching allied with the more conservative art-educational practices prevalent in the other Scottish art colleges, yet also looked to the European avant-garde. In addition, Munnoch, like Harcourt, encouraged students to develop their own creative visions and thereby provided the foundation for many diverse artistic careers.

Henry Daniel, Governor 1926–8

Today, Henry Daniel shares Munnoch's situation as an artist who was seen as a promising talent during his lifetime, but now remains a relatively obscure figure. Daniel was trained at the Slade School in London and, at the time of his appointment to the College, was a drawing teacher at Trinity College Glenalmond, an elite public boarding school for boys, and a regular exhibitor at the Royal Scottish Academy of Art and Architecture.[66] Although continued economic difficulties for the College meant that Daniel only had a short time to implement his own approach, his impact was still evident. He valued the practice of life drawing, something that would have been particularly important to his own education at the Slade, and sought to increase the frequency of this activity at the College.[67] In addition to passing on his dedication to draughtsmanship, he also shared his affinity with painting the landscape.

In a review of Daniel's work at the 1935 Royal Academy Exhibition, the *Evening Telegraph* complimented him as an artist who: 'reveals in all his work a love of nature and an ability to capture her moods and charms'.[68] His ability to do so is exemplified by his pastel of Hospitalfield. By leading the eye through a curving row of trees, whose empty branches are contrasted with groupings of flowering daffodils, Daniel presented a view that captured the arrival of spring. A sense of the expectant growth and vitality of the landscape was further suggested by the soft surface Daniel achieved when depicting the grassy field and the accentuated roundness of the forms of Hospitalfield House. This treatment of the landscape corresponds with that which appears in a later work of his former student Charles Christie Ruxton (1900–1971).[69] In Ruxton's 1968 work, *The Ruin*, found in the collection of Angus Council, Ruxton applied a sensitivity to light and shade similar to that featured in Daniel's pastel, but intensified the contrast to create a more dramatic atmosphere. By combining this greater contrast with a darker, more restricted palette, Ruxton imbued his landscape with a sense of brooding and mystery.

Another student who benefited from Daniel's encouragement to engage with the landscape surrounding Hospitalfield was Joseph Webb, ARE (1908–1962), who enrolled in 1925. This training gave him the technical foundation to develop his talent for etching and, in 1930, he was elected to the Royal Society of Painter Etchers. No doubt having access to the varied landscape of Arbroath helped him develop his observational and interpretive skills. Two of his student etchings, both entitled *Hospitalfield Farm* (figs 2.15 & 2.16), exemplify his growing skills of draughtsmanship. The progression from simple line drawing to intricate cross-hatching as the image unfolds in proximity to the viewer in *Hospitalfield Farm* has a delicacy and rhythm that reflect Webb's early command of the medium. The more developed etching of *Hospitalfield Farm* is particularly representative of his ability to convey a sense of atmosphere and drama that captures the viewer's imagination through skilful use of light and shadow, a quality that would become characteristic of his later work.[70]

Forces of change

Daniel's years at the College, while productive, would have also been influenced by an undercurrent of uncertainty. Throughout the 1920s, the Hospitalfield estate's debts mounted. With the estate unable to recover from post-war recession and therefore unable to continue to fund the College, a new plan was needed.[72] Deciding what this plan would be was not a straightforward process for the Trustees. A series of debates and disagreements, each influenced by the Trustees' various personal and professional opinions, lasted from 1924 until 1935.

One of the most influential personalities in the controversy surrounding the future of the College was the President of the Royal Scottish Academy of Art and Architecture (RSA), the architect George Washington Browne. Upon becoming President, Browne refused to join the Trustees, believing the College was financially defunct and outdated in its educational approach. With his opinion informed by his experience as a faculty member of Edinburgh College of Art, he argued in a series of letters to the Trustees that students benefited from having: 'a specially qualified teacher for each subject, amid the breezy atmosphere of hundreds of fellow students with their varied outlook on life ... To segregate a small handful of students ... with a single mentor ... is to enclose them within a circle so small ... and stifle rather than develop whatever abilities they start with.'[73]

Browne's colleague James Paterson, the Secretary of the RSA, had been an influential member of the Trustees for several years.[74] Paterson also believed that an Edinburgh education could benefit a young painter's career, but for reasons that differed from the arguments Browne presented. Despite becoming a distinguished painter as one of the 'Glasgow School' or 'Glasgow Boys', Paterson had struggled for admission to the RSA because of the preference shown to those educated and working in Edinburgh.[75] It is likely he felt that, by supporting the petition to the Court of Session to close the College, sell Hospitalfield and use the resulting funds to support a Scheme

FROM THE ALLAN-FRASER ART COLLEGE
TO THE PATRICK ALLAN-FRASER TRUST SCHEME

1924: Architect George Washington Browne is elected President of the Royal Scottish Academy of Art and Architecture (RSA) and refuses to join the Trustees.

1924–7: Debate among the Trustees as to the future of the College.

1926: Governor Peter Munnoch dies of a heart attack. Henry Daniel is appointed Governor.

1927: The majority of Trustees petition the Court of Session to dissolve the College and sell the Hospitalfield estate and all its assets so the resulting funds can be transferred to the RSA to be applied under a new scheme to establish studios in Edinburgh for recent art graduates. The only dissenting Trustee is the Provost of Arbroath, Alexander Maclaren Robertson, whose counter-petitions proposed that Hospitalfield remain the site of the College.

1928: The last students leave Hospitalfield. Henry Daniel and his wife remain as caretakers until 1935.

1929: The Court of Session rejects the Trustees' proposal, believing it to be too radical a change from Allan-Fraser's bequest and that other solutions may be possible.

1929–31: With the approval of the Court of Session, the Trustees sell land and moveable assets to raise money to reopen the College.

1933: The Scottish Education Department (SED) mandates that all Educational Endowments be reviewed. The College (still closed) is audited and declared unfit to reopen as a four-year independent art school.

1933–5: A new scheme of art education at Hospitalfield is formulated by the Trustees with recommendations from the SED.

1935: The Patrick Allan-Fraser Trust Scheme is approved by Parliament.

1937: The first students are admitted under the Patrick Allan-Fraser Trust Scheme.[71]

FIG. 2.15

Joseph Webb, Hospitalfield Farm, c.*1925–35*

etching on white laid paper, 18.5 x 28.4 cm / Aberystwyth University School of Art Museum and Galleries
(purchased 2005 from Beryl Gascoigne and Jane Furst with grant aid from the V&A and Art Fund)
© the artist's estate, all rights reserved / image courtesy of Aberystwyth University, 2017

FIG. 2.16

Joseph Webb, Hospitalfield Farm, c.*1925–35*

etching on white laid paper, 12.7 x 17.5 cm / Aberystwyth University School of Art Museum and Galleries
(purchased 2005 from Beryl Gascoigne and Jane Furst with grant aid from the V&A and Art Fund)
© the artist's estate, all rights reserved / image courtesy of Aberystwyth University, 2017

run by the RSA to establish new Edinburgh studios, he was giving young artists an opportunity that had not been available to him. As a young man, Paterson believed that the French atelier was the best source of art education. Having experienced the artistic world of Paris for himself, he wrote in his 1888 *Scottish Art Review* article that the rigours of the atelier were usually far more demanding than those of 'any art school in Great Britain'.[76] If faced with the dilemma about the College's future, the younger Paterson may have suggested Hospitalfield be sold to establish scholarships for art students to study abroad or to form a Scottish enclave in Paris. It is possible the actions of the more mature Paterson reveal a change of heart and that, over time, he felt that the standard for British art education had improved. It is equally probable that the prospect of managing a new well-funded Scheme on behalf of the Academy was too tempting an opportunity to let pass.

While Browne's and Paterson's support of the petition had elements of professional bias, the opposition to their proposition, presented by Trustee Alexander Maclaren Robertson, was likewise influenced by his position. As Provost of Arbroath, Robertson had the town's interests, and no doubt his own reputation, in mind when he argued that the College should remain because of its positive impact on the lives of its students and the cultural and economic life of Arbroath. Munnoch, and later Daniel, also had a professional stake in the debate, as the closure of the College would have meant the loss of their job. It was Munnoch and Daniel, however, who, more than any of the Trustees, had the most relevant insight into the effectiveness and value of the education the College provided. In support of its preservation Munnoch argued, 'The works of the Old Masters, works that are studied today as examples, were produced before the establishment of Art Schools at all, when artists were trained as pupils or apprentices under the mind of one man.' He added further support to his argument by citing the continued success of the small-scale master-apprentice system, referencing its continued application in France and its historic application under Robert Scott Lauder at Edinburgh's Trustees' Academy.[77] For Daniel, it was the College's free education that he felt must continue: 'So far as I know there is not an institution in the kingdom except Hospitalfield which enables young men not having sufficient means of their own to obtain an art education and at the same time provides them with means of subsistence.'[78]

While the debate about the College's future was influenced by these differing personal and professional perspectives, in many ways it was also reflective of cultural and educational changes throughout Scotland. The original mission of the College had aligned with the culture of Victorian philanthropy, yet within the climate of post-war austerity, its aims and provisions seemed increasingly excessive and frivolous. Without a curriculum approved by the SED, the College was also no longer in line with the current educational standards to which Browne alluded. While the Court of Session prevented the sale of Hospitalfield and suggested the College may still have a future, it was the SED that would ultimately determine that it would never reopen.

A few months after the death of Patrick Allan-Fraser, *The Isle of Man Times and General Advertiser* optimistically predicted: 'It is impossible to over-estimate the effect on Scottish art which the "Patrick Allan Fraser Institute" will exercise in another generation or so.'[79] Did the closure of the College mean that it failed to live up to the high hopes for Patrick Allan-Fraser's bequest? Certainly, the College was never a financial success. Limited funds had consistently narrowed the scope of the College's enrolment and educational offerings. The bequest had envisioned thirty students living and working at Hospitalfield. During its first two years, the College hosted 26 students, but in subsequent years, enrolment was limited to a maximum

FIG. 2.17

Aerial photograph of Hospitalfield House, Arbroath, 1932

of ten students. In addition, Patrick outlined that the school would 'assist and encourage young men in following out one or more of the Professions of Painter, Sculptor, Carver in Wood, Architect, or Engraver'.[80] The College never offered wood-carving and, rather than combining fine and applied art education, primarily emphasised fine art practices of drawing and painting. It is likely that with better financial management, the College could have more closely aligned with the original bequest. Even if this was achieved, it is doubtful that the Hospitalfield estate could have continued to support the College after its fiscal decline in the 1920s or that the College could have survived the widespread changes in art education.

Despite its financial challenges and smaller scale and scope, the College can still be considered significant in its contribution to British art education and art. Its residential nature, country setting and master-apprentice teaching dynamic presented an alternative model to the larger urban art-educational institutions of Scotland. Additionally, the College's students, whose economic situations meant they would have struggled to begin an artistic career, benefited from a free four-year art education. That the work of approximately one-third of the 75 students who enrolled are, today, in British public art collections is evidence of the effectiveness of the education they received. Furthermore, that many more former students made careers in the arts in Scotland, England and beyond speaks to its widespread influence. Lastly, the College carried out and preserved Patrick and Elizabeth's intention that Hospitalfield remain a site devoted to the cultivation of art and artists. Although the specific mission of Hospitalfield would be altered with the formation of the new Patrick Allan-Fraser Trust Scheme of 1935, it would be this core principle that would enable this site in Arbroath to continue to impact art on a local to international scale.

3

The era of artist-wardens
The Patrick Allan-Fraser Trust Scheme 1935–54

SUMMARY OF THE PATRICK ALLAN-FRASER TRUST SCHEME OF 1935

- *Hospitalfield would host a select number of graduates from each of the four Scottish art colleges in Aberdeen, Dundee, Edinburgh and Glasgow.*
- *Students would be chosen by their respective institutions, with the primary requirement being that a candidate was a 'genuine and meritorious student of drawing and painting'.[1]*
- *An experienced artist and teacher would be appointed as Warden, to be resident at Hospitalfield and responsible for the property and the students. The Warden would provide guidance rather than formal teaching for the students.*
- *The Trustees prior to 1935 would become ex-officio members, with the primary body of Trustees formed of four elected representatives, one from each of the four Scottish art colleges.*
- *The duration of and fee for the students' residencies would be left to the discretion of the Trustees.[2]*

The closure of the College did not mean the end of artistic activity at Hospitalfield. Instead, the Patrick Allan-Fraser Trust Scheme of 1935 ushered in a new era.[3] Under the Scheme, Hospitalfield was no longer the site of an independent art college, but hosted a programme of continuing education that was integrated into the national higher education framework. Each year, representatives of Scotland's four art-educational institutions of the time, Edinburgh College of Art, Dundee College of Art, Glasgow School of Art and Gray's School of Art in Aberdeen, nominated a select number of drawing and painting students to spend a period of residency at Hospitalfield under the direction of an experienced artist and teacher.[4] While the Scheme's residential nature meant that, at first, it retained the Allan-Fraser Art College's male-only policy, by 1940, female students were allowed to attend.

The Scheme augmented the educational experience of students from the Aberdeen, Dundee, Edinburgh and Glasgow institutions in three ways. Firstly, as an article in *The Scotsman* explained: 'a feature of the scheme is that the students are left almost entirely to their own initiative. There is no fixed and arranged timetable or curriculum.'[5] This contrasted with the structured curricula of the art colleges and allowed students to transition from completing assigned work to generating their own individual practices.[6] Secondly, the Scheme provided the opportunity for talented graduates to meet and work alongside their contemporaries from the other art colleges. This enabled ideas and techniques to be exchanged and fostered a sense of community. Lastly, the Scheme, like the College that preceded it, viewed the varied visual environment of Hospitalfield's surroundings as an asset for student learning. As landscape painting was not a mainstay of the Scottish art colleges' curricula, which focused upon the figure, still-life and composition, students could explore this genre through the Scheme.

The intended outcomes of providing a time of independence, an artistic community and an opportunity to engage with a stimulating visual environment continually manifested themselves throughout the remainder of the twentieth century at Hospitalfield. The ways in which they did were, however, greatly influenced by the Warden.

It was not until two years after the Scheme was approved by Parliament in 1935 that the first Warden arrived at Hospitalfield. This was James Cowie, RSA (1886–1956), who served from 1937 to 1948. His successor was Ian Fleming, who held the position from 1948 to 1954. Cowie and Fleming were among the most significant artists and teachers of Scotland's twentieth century,[7] with reputations whose development was intrinsically connected to their periods as Warden. At Hospitalfield, both artists produced significant bodies of work and influenced the artistic development of many of the student residents through their advice and examples. As Cowie and Fleming utilised their role in a similar way, and this role would afterwards change in character, their time of leadership can, in hindsight, be viewed as the era of the 'Artist-Wardens'.

FIG. 3.1
James Cowie, Evening Star, *c.1940—4*

oil on canvas, 137.5 x 133.4 cm / Aberdeen Art Gallery & Museums Collections, Aberdeen (purchased in 1954 with income from the Macdonald Bequest)

Warden James Cowie: his artwork 1937–48

The art of James Cowie was both a response to the artistic context in which he trained and worked, and a product of his uniquely personal vision and practice. The foundation of his art education was laid at Glasgow School of Art from 1912 to 1914. There he refined his draughtsmanship and learned the process of constructing a final composition from numerous observed studies. These skills became the fundamental elements of the artistic practice that developed throughout his career. The application of this process can be seen by comparing studies with the final product, for example the *c.*1940–4 Hospitalfield-period painting *Evening Star* (fig. 3.1). The studies for this (figs 3.2–3.3), which capture the tones and textures of the rock formation in Arbroath's Seaton cliffs known as the Needle's E'e [Eye],[8] exemplify his facility in translating the world around him into line and form. Creating a realistic copy from nature, however, was only one step in an interpretive process. Comparing the shape of the opening of the Needle's E'e in the study with that of the final painting reveals how Cowie purposefully manipulated this form to create space for the nude figures and allow a view to the beach below.

FIG. 3.2

James Cowie, Rock *(study for* Evening Star*)*

FIG. 3.3
James Cowie, Rocks *(study for* Evening Star*)*

pencil on paper 37.1 x 32.5 cm / Aberdeen Art Gallery & Museums Collections, Aberdeen (purchased in 1983)
© the artist's estate, all rights reserved / image courtesy of Aberdeen Art Gallery & Museums, 2017

Cowie's continued use of the techniques he learned as a student was not the result of unquestioningly following tradition, but a deliberate decision. The lengthy process from studies to final composition allowed him time to achieve the type of aesthetic clarity he believed to be of stylistic value. Qualities of linearity, crisp rendering and complex, multi-layered compositions are evident in paintings throughout his career; from work created between 1915 and 1935, when he taught at the Bellshill Academy located outside Glasgow, through to his brief period from 1935 to 1937 at Gray's School of Art in Aberdeen and his time at Hospitalfield. This style related to that of his former GSA classmates and artistic contemporaries, such as Robert Sivell and Archibald McGlashan. A similar aesthetic is also evident in the work of later GSA students James McIntosh Patrick and Edward Baird who, like Cowie, settled on Scotland's

FIG. 3.4
James Cowie

Angus Council Collections managed by ANGUSalive Museums, Galleries & Archives / image courtesy of Angus Council, 2017

northeast coast.[9] In hindsight, these artists can be considered as forming an aesthetic subculture within Scottish painting, which originated in Glasgow and migrated to the northeast between Dundee and Aberdeen.

While Cowie's aesthetic related to a subset of his contemporaries and remained relatively constant throughout his career, the conceptual aspects of his paintings grew increasingly complex and individual at Hospitalfield. His ideas are, perhaps, most comprehensively distilled in his 1937–47 self-portrait, *The Blue Shirt* (fig. 3.5). The composition of *The Blue Shirt* echoed that of Nicolas Poussin's 1650 *Self-portrait* and further reference to Poussin was made through the inclusion of his *c.*1630 *The Inspiration of the Epic Poet* in the background.[10] Poussin reinvented the values of Classical art – logic, order and beauty in proportion – within seventeenth-century French painting. Cowie's self-portrait provides several visual cues that suggest that he intended to follow this model within the context of twentieth-century Scotland. For instance, Cowie simplified the composition of *The Inspiration of the Epic Poet* so that the laurel crown that appears within his version of that painting was situated above his own head; in addition, he positioned himself so as to sit in front of the Poussin painting – all of which asserts that he was the next in line with regard to this artistic tradition.

Further evidence of the ways in which Cowie sought to reinvent Classical values within modern painting can be found in the development of his imagery from earlier works to those of his Hospitalfield period. As in his self-portrait, the two young art students in his 1934–5 *Two Schoolgirls* are positioned in a way that suggests the progression of an artistic lineage, whose beginning is embodied by the cast of the ancient Greek statue *Discobolus* that stands behind them. A similar concept is also expressed in Cowie's 1934 *Falling Leaves*, in which the cast of Michelangelo's *Dawn*[11] – which harks back to the Italian Renaissance, the rebirth of Classical values – presides over the two art students. In Hospitalfield paintings by Cowie such as *Evening Star* and *Composition* (fig. 3.6), references to Classical art, and to art forms that followed and expanded upon this tradition, continually appear. By juxtaposing images like Ingres' *Grande Odalisque* or Greek sculptures with the landscape of Arbroath within these paintings, Cowie visually and symbolically connected the Classical tradition with his own time and place.

By evoking the work of Paul Cézanne, Cowie further affirmed his connection to a neoclassical artistic lineage. Cézanne famously sought to *refaire Poussin sur nature*[12] – redo Poussin after nature. Cowie's practice of looking to Classical art, but also looking to nature to make studies consistently from the world around him, aligned with Cézanne's practice. Cowie reminded the viewer of this frequently by depicting Classical casts and statues in front of a window, as in *Set Square* (fig. 5.11), or directly against the landscape, as in *Composition*. Cowie also incorporated Cézanne's method of manipulating perspective in his work. This appears subtly in paintings like *The Looking Glass* (fig. 3.7), in which the angle of the bowl at one end of the table seems to be depicted from a different vantage point to the curve of the vase at the other end. In other paintings, such as *Composition*, which has endless layers of images, objects and reflections, Cowie surpassed Cézanne's use of this technique by completely disorienting any sense of pictorial perspective.

Yet Cowie not only looked to the past for inspiration. Other aspects of his visual language and conceptual concerns related to the metaphysical painters of his era. Scottish contemporary Edward Baird, English painters like Edward Wadsworth and Paul Nash, and European artists such as Giorgio de Chirico, like Cowie, used visual juxtapositions to create unsettling and challenging enigmas. These artists achieved this by employing a clear and precise aesthetic, which suggested realism, to construct compositions that brought together

James Cowie, The Blue Shirt, *1937–47*

oil on canvas, 66 x 55.5 cm / University of Edinburgh Art Collection, Edinburgh: EU0776 (purchased by the University Pictures Committee, 1974)

FIG. 3.6

James Cowie, Composition, *1947*

oil on wood, 46.3 x 45.5 cm / National Galleries of Scotland, Edinburgh (bequested by Sir William Oliphant Hutchison, 1970)
© the artist's estate, all rights reserved / image courtesy of National Galleries of Scotland, 2017

'[*Art is*] *The expression of an idea which has the power of evoking emotion. What moves in nature may be made to move in the same way when nature is copied. This at the present stage in art history (we are suffering from a surfeit of impressionism or the lyrical) is to me not enough for a picture, which must be an idea, a concept built of much that in its total combination it would never be possible to see and to copy.*'[13]

'*The artist of today was tired of the work of art which was the vehicle of individual feeling ... It meant that the artist today was tired of the stress which his predecessors had laid upon spontaneity in art ... the artist today had thrown overboard completely the notion that his picture must resemble nature in its physical aspects and had permitted himself a freedom in the use of language that had seldom been enjoyed in art.*'[14]

'*Painting is not an end in itself, but a means to an end — a language to convey ideas.*'[15]

seemingly unreal combinations of objects, figures and landscapes.

Of Cowie's work, T. Elder Dickson concluded in his 1951 exhibition review for *The Scotsman*: 'All that is best in traditional art is represented in his work, while he uses a modern idiom of great refinement and polish ... all bespeak a mind of rare awareness and quality.'[16] Through his artistic process, technical skill and imagery Cowie connected with the Classical tradition. Using elements of visual language from modernists like Cézanne and his contemporaries concerned with metaphysical painting, he extended and expanded the artistic lineage of neoclassicism. All this he did using art objects in his Hospitalfield studio and the landscapes of Arbroath.

Warden James Cowie: his influence 1937–48

Hospitalfield provided Cowie with the visual environment, the time and the facilities to develop his imagery, his aesthetic and his ideas. It also gave him the opportunity to transfer his knowledge and beliefs about art to the next generation of young Scottish painters. Just as the artistic learning and personal growth of his pupils became the subject of many paintings from his period at the Bellshill Academy, his 1938–41 *An Outdoor School of Painting* (fig. 3.9) and c.1946–7 *Studio Interior* (fig. 3.8) record the student-Warden dynamic at Hospitalfield. Both works capture how Cowie sought to encourage the students to adopt practices that he believed benefited the development of young artists — practices which happened to be similar to his own.

In the foreground of *An Outdoor School of Painting* are several figures engaged in activities Cowie advocated: making studies from nature, contemplating and learning from the Classical tradition of the Old Masters (represented by the presence of nude figures in the background). Applying the teachings he encouraged within his own painting, Cowie based the recurrent male figure in *Outdoor School* on studies he had made of Waistel Cooper, a young artist from Ayr Academy who attended the official Scheme as an external student and went on to become a potter.[17] The male student with his back towards the viewer was based on artist Robert MacBryde, while the seated female figure was based on Cowie's eldest daughter Ruth and the standing female figure on his youngest daughter Barbara.[18]

In the background, several nude figures appear in the landscape. These evoke the Classical tradition Cowie reinvented while suggesting his hope that his students would do the same. Combining these elements, this painting illustrated his vision for Hospitalfield. In a report to the Trustees, Cowie relayed how he encouraged the students to complete 'a composition embodying one or two figures preferably in an outdoor setting the material of which could be supplied by their immediate surroundings',[19] a final product embodied by and demonstrated in *An Outdoor School of Painting*.

Further indication of Cowie's desire to pass on aspects of his practice to his students is found in *Studio Interior*. As in *An Outdoor School of Painting*, the students in *Studio Interior* engage in processes Cowie supported, such as drawing from life and making studies for a final composition. In this image, however, Cowie depicted himself working beside his students. He further asserted his presence in *Studio Interior* by compositionally surrounding the students with his own work. In the foreground is the sculpture of his own making which featured in his 1947 *Composition*, c.1940 *Fantasy with Figures and Easels* and 1946 *Noon*. In the background is his 1933 *Nude* as well as his 1940–4 *Evening Star*, which he believed to be his: 'most potent and profound statement'.[20]

It is unsurprising that such a forceful presence yielded divergent reactions among the students. Epitomising one side of this spectrum of response was that of the artist, art writer and critic Cordelia Oliver, who attended Hospitalfield

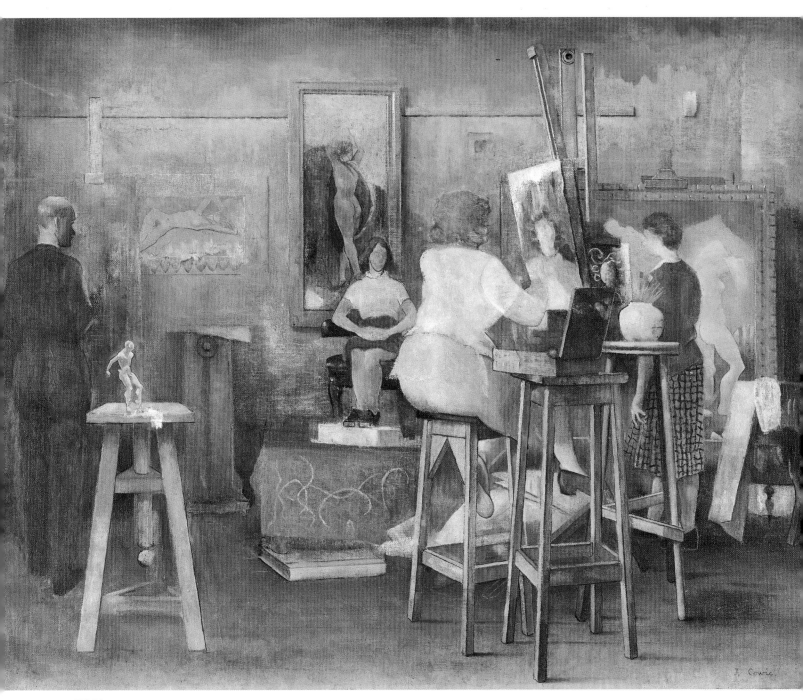

FIG. 3.8
James Cowie, Studio Interior, *1946–7*

oil on canvas, 71.1 x 91.4 cm / private collection, Scotland / © the artist's estate, all rights reserved / image courtesy of The Fine Art Society in Edinburgh, 2017

FIG. 3.9

James Cowie, An Outdoor School of Painting, *1938—41*

oil on canvas, 86.4 x 165.1 cm / Tate (purchased 1983) / © the artist's estate, all rights reserved / image © Tate, London 2017

in 1944 from Glasgow School of Art. Her characterisation of Cowie in her 1980 book *James Cowie* set the precedent for Cowie to be thought of as an opinionated, arrogant, argumentative teacher:

> The Cowie I knew was a teacher with whom, more than occasionally, I agreed to differ, but one on whose mordant, not to say opinionated mind, I honed the edge of my own intellect ... The man who refused to suffer fools gladly was also the man who, on occasion, was known to swallow flattery. It is true that he tended to bully the timorous, and that what he enjoyed most was a student with spunk enough to 'come back' at him.[21]

MORRIS GRASSIE RECALLS JAMES COWIE

Morris Grassie (b.1931) was born and raised in Arbroath and his first memory of Hospitalfield was formed at the age of eight. Cowie, a lover of music as well as art, had heard Grassie's neighbour Tom Strachan perform on the piano and invited him to Hospitalfield to play. One Sunday morning, the two boys cycled to Hospitalfield. While Strachan played Brahms, Grassie had a conversation that would begin an artistic journey. Of this occasion Grassie recalled:

Mr Cowie said to me: What's it you do?
MG: Well I'm not an artist, but I like drawing and painting.
JC: Oh, well have you got any drawings?
MG: No, I've not got anything.
JC: Well if you're going to come out here every Sunday, you've got to bring drawings. What do you use?
MG: Well I like pencil actually.
JC: Oh right, do you know anything about pencils?
[MG: Well a pencil's a pencil — I thought!]
JC: Show me the pencil you've got.
[MG: I had this pencil, just an ordinary pencil.]
JC: My goodness me! I'll give you some pencils.
[MG: And he gave me a set of pencils from 5H right the way down to B and from B all the way up to 6B so there was a total range.]
JC: Now I'll also give you a sharpener as well. They must all be needle sharp. You draw with the point, you don't draw with the side, you draw with the point. Okay? Now next week I want you to come back and you'll do a fishing boat, some trees and a house. That's your target, come back next week.[24]

Grassie's connection to Hospitalfield evolved from that day forward. Throughout his art education, he frequented the Hospitalfield studios to engage with the student residents, recalling that: 'the community and the friendship and the way they helped one another was extremely exciting for me as a young person.'[25] After achieving his diploma at Dundee College of Art, Grassie then returned to Hospitalfield under the Scheme in 1952 and 1953 (under the Wardenship of Ian Fleming). Together, his experiences at Hospitalfield were formative ones upon which his life-long career in art and education were built.

In contrast, there are many accounts of Cowie that provide insight into other aspects of his nature — indicating his humility, his generosity and his genuine desire to assist others on their artistic journey. For instance, Glasgow School of Art's Director Douglas Percy Bliss, who would have met Cowie frequently as a Hospitalfield Trustee, stated in his review of Cowie's one-man show in 1947 that: 'Mr Cowie was one of the most distinguished artists in Scotland, and quite incurably modest.'[22] That Cowie, in his annual report from 1941, praised the students by stating, 'Never I think have we had a year where students worked more harmoniously and with greater enthusiasm',[23] reveals that he valued a content and productive working environment at Hospitalfield rather than one of conflict.

His devotion to promoting the development of young artists was also undeniable as he frequently went above and beyond his remit as Warden to engage with aspiring artists in the community of Arbroath. He allowed several servicemen and members of their families stationed at a nearby Air Force base to spend their time on leave drawing and painting at Hospitalfield. He was instrumental in the re-establishment of the Arbroath Art Society[26] in 1946 and assisted the Society by arranging a programme of talks, events, an annual members' exhibition and several exhibitions curated by the recently formed Committee for the Encouragement of Music and the Arts.

Through his involvement with the Arbroath Art Society, Hospitalfield's link to the artistic life of Arbroath grew stronger. Hospitalfield students participated in the Society and young members, encouraged to join the Society by Arbroath art master (and future Warden) William Reid, were given opportunities to visit and work at Hospitalfield. Among these were Joan Cuthill, Euphemia Findlay, George Grassie, Morris Grassie, William Littlejohn, RSA, RSW, Angus Neil and Alexander Robbie, each of whom contributed to the artistic life of Scotland as artists and teachers.

The varying characterisations of Cowie suggest a multi-faceted, nuanced individual who had a wide range of effects upon the artists he encountered. Due to this spectrum of response, tracing his level of influence as an artist on the students at Hospitalfield involves considering the interaction between the artistic affinities and interpersonal relationships of the students and their Warden. For example, Robert Colquhoun (1914–1962) and Robert MacBryde (1913–1966), 'The Two Roberts', so called because of their connection in art and life, attended Hospitalfield in 1938 and were notoriously rebellious against Cowie's authority.[27] Cowie's eldest daughter Ruth, when reflecting upon the seven years she spent at Hospitalfield, recalled that: 'it was clear that their work and ideas were alien to my father, though I think he struggled to understand them.'[28] Given this dynamic, it is unlikely, as some have conjectured,[29] that Cowie's influence can be seen in the linear draughtsmanship of their drawings from this period. It is more likely that this skill was acquired earlier at the Glasgow School of Art through the example of their teacher and friend Ian Fleming (who would become Warden). While Cowie's approach caused Colquhoun and MacBryde to have, as Colquhoun described in a letter to Ian Fleming, 'a stiff time up here',[30] their spell at Hospitalfield offered other benefits. It was a precious opportunity to continue making work following art school in an environment free of the financial pressure they would soon experience. It was also where they met Irish-born Patrick Hennessy, RHA (1915–1980), who had grown up in Arbroath and would officially attend Hospitalfield as a student from Dundee in 1939. This friendship continued after Hospitalfield as they travelled through France together later that year. In 1946, the Roberts spent time in County Cork, Ireland, where Hennessy had settled and had begun to establish himself as an artist through his unique modernist-realist paintings. There Colquhoun gathered imagery that inspired a series of paintings and monotypes.

When Hennessy attended Hospitalfield as a selected student from Dundee College of Art, he, like his friends, formed a fractious dynamic with Cowie, which culminated in his early departure. This was also the case for Hennessy's Hospitalfield and Dundee contemporary Alexander Allan, RSW (1914–1972). Ironically, there are many similarities between Hennessy, Allan and Cowie's work. Hennessy's c.1940 Old Kinsale (fig. 3.10) has a clarity of handling that consistently characterised Cowie's work. In Old Kinsale, as in Cowie's paintings like Evening Star, this stylistic quality, which usually denotes an artist's attempt to accurately represent reality, creates a sense of mystery and wonderment when used to portray an enigmatic scene. Both paintings juxtapose recognisable places with figures whose presence destabilises the reality suggested by the settings. Just as Evening Star brought nude figures to the sandstone cliffs of Arbroath, in Old Kinsale, the viewer is given a glimpse of the Irish coastal town through a window on whose recess rests the hand of a cloaked figure. In this way, Cowie and Hennessy created metaphysical paintings that demanded the continual contemplation of their unsolvable riddles.

There is an even more timely and pointed brooding in the darkened landscape of Allan's c.1939 Fantastic Landscape (fig. 3.11). Like many of Cowie's Hospitalfield still-lifes, this picture introduces a variety of objects in the foreground, which hover from a high vantage point above the countryside beyond, based on Glen Clova in Angus. This type of composition challenges the viewer to reconcile the disorienting visual relationship between the combination of disparate elements, over which a distress flare bursts in the sky — in hindsight serving as a prophetic symbol of the years of war to follow.[31]

Further stylistic similarities between Cowie's and Allan's work are evident in Allan's inclusion of a picture within a picture. Like the easels in Cowie's Evening Star or mirror in The Looking Glass, the ambiguous shape, perhaps a canvas or decorative screen, in Fantastic Landscape introduces an image that is nested within the greater image of the painting. These elements also add further compositional layers to the already visually and conceptually complex painting.

FIG. 3.10

Patrick Hennessy, Old Kinsale, c.*1940*

oil on canvas, 76 x 50.5 cm / Crawford Art Gallery, Cork (Gibson Fund purchase from the artist, 1940)

FIG. 3.11

Alexander Allan, Fantastic Landscape, c.*1939*

oil on board, 34 x 44.7 cm / Dundee City Council: Dundee's Art Galleries and Museums (Scottish Arts Council Collection bequest, 1998)
© the artist's estate, all rights reserved / image courtesy of Dundee City Council, 2017

While conflicts of personality make identifying influence between the Warden and these students questionable, the similarities in their work can be interpreted as evidence of a more pervasive aesthetic culture in the northeast of Scotland. Here artists like Robert Sivell in Aberdeen, Edward Baird in Montrose, Cowie in Arbroath and James McIntosh Patrick in Dundee created precise, clear and compositionally focused paintings.

The experiences of John Laurie (1916–1972) and Charles Pulsford, ARSA (1912–1989), provide a foil to those of Colquhoun, MacBryde, Hennessy and Allan. Laurie and Pulsford not only productively co-existed with Cowie, but their work shows distinctive evidence of his influence. Laurie first attended Hospitalfield in 1938 from Glasgow School of Art. That he returned in 1939 and 1940 is indicative of the strength of Cowie's formative influence. This is also evident from the style and imagery of his 1939 *Interested and Disinterested*. Its crispness of rendering and multi-layered composition is akin to Cowie's aesthetic, while its subject, two young artists at work surrounded by art room objects in a landscape, contains many of Cowie's common motifs. Laurie's continued regard for Cowie as well as his understanding of his practice, is captured in his 1947 *Portrait of James Cowie*. In this image, Laurie not only conveys an essence of Cowie the artist by depicting him with his work, but also creates the portrait in a style akin to Cowie's own.

RAY HOWARD-JONES AT HOSPITALFIELD

Rosemary, known as Ray, Howard-Jones (1903–1996) was among a small number of students to take part as external participants in the artistic community at Hospitalfield. She attended Hospitalfield in 1946, after training at the Slade and serving as a War Artist recording the Normandy Landing preparations.

Her 1945–6 painting Homage to James Cowie *(fig. 3.12) is a fusion of Cowie's influence with her own style. As in many of Cowie's still-life compositions, her* Homage *presents a carefully rendered still-life grouping in the foreground against a landscape. While Cowie's images of still-life objects presiding over the countryside only allude to a human presence, the hands that extend into the foreground of Howard-Jones' painting directly assert a presence. The still-life grouping in* Homage *also takes up less compositional space than is typically seen in works by Cowie. This creates a larger mid-ground where Howard-Jones displayed the softer style of rendering and freer brushwork that was her own stylistic affinity. Referred to by the artist and teacher Philip Wilson Steer as 'the best colourist the Slade ever produced',[32] Howard-Jones also utilised her sensitivity regarding colour in* Homage *by increasing the intensity of Cowie's characteristically cool palette with deeper, more vibrant blues.*

After Hospitalfield, Howard-Jones returned to London and continued to devote herself to painting, exhibiting in the UK and abroad throughout her long and productive career. Homage to James Cowie *now serves as a record of her time at Hospitalfield, the artistic exchanges that took place and the way Hospitalfield connected artists of varying educational backgrounds, life experiences and artistic affinities.[33]*

In 1939, Charles Pulsford attended Hospitalfield from Edinburgh College of Art and his *Untitled (Surrealist Townscape)* (fig. 3.14), from the same year, while less directly derivative of Cowie's work than Laurie's, still exhibits qualities that suggest the Warden's influence. The isolation and intense inner life of Pulsford's figures, which challenge viewers to reconcile the meaning of their relationship with the objects, the city street, and one another, echo the effect of Cowie's compositions. Although Pulsford spent the majority of his later career experimenting with abstraction, his *Untitled* is one of a series of works that marked an intersection between his and Cowie's artistic affinities.

Still Life by Nita Begg (1920–2011) (fig. 3.13), who attended Hospitalfield in 1947 from Glasgow School of Art, provides evidence that a middle ground between rebellion and agreement was possible. The still-life was set up for Begg to paint by Cowie and, certainly, its subject of art room objects contrasted by a screen-like geometric form are consistent with Cowie's own compositions of this period. Cowie's guiding force can also be seen in the painting's cool, restricted palette and ambiguous visual space. In her freer and looser handling of paint Begg does, however, distinguish her work from Cowie's clear, linear paintings. The painterly quality evident in *Still Life*, particularly in the background, was not only characteristic of the bolder approach the Glasgow faculty encouraged, but was a feature that would continue to define Begg's later work. By integrating elements characteristic of Cowie's work with her own style, Begg showed her willingness to learn, while also asserting her independence.

Cowie's 1947 report to the Trustees indicates that the willingness of Begg and her fellow students, along with their talent and dedication, inspired him to share his teachings about art:

FIG. 3.12

Ray Howard-Jones, Homage to James Cowie, *1945–6*

oil on hardboard, 71.2 x 91.5 cm / Glasgow Museums and Libraries Collections (purchased 1972) / © the artist's estate, all rights reserved / image © CSG CIC Glasgow Museums and Libraries Collections

It has been often noticeable, naturally enough perhaps, that students trained in the same school of art show too much sameness in the work they produce. This year three of the above students were trained in the Glasgow School of Art but do not exhibit this characteristic in the work they have done. Nothing could be more marked than the widely different points of reference in painting of Miss Eardley, Miss Begg and Mr. Gallacher. Combined with the seriousness with which these have all worked this has made for an interest in teaching more than usual. In its different way the work of each is interesting, promising and capable of, perhaps, great development.[34]

In hindsight, Cowie's statement seems prophetic, as all three students from Glasgow School of Art – Nita Begg, William Gallacher (1920–1978), whom Begg later married, and Joan Eardley, RSA (1921–1963) – became significant contributors to Scottish art. Cowie's reflection also provides a foil for the fractious dynamic between Cowie and Eardley, which is often described.[35] Certainly, there was a difference in approach to drawing and painting between Cowie and Eardley. Where Cowie would have used a thin, delicate line, Eardley would have applied a thick, expressive stroke. When Cowie would labour over a painting for years, Eardley would work quickly *en plein air*, allowing spontaneity and chance to leaves their marks. There would also have been healthy debate on this topic, as evidenced by Eardley's letter to fellow artist and Glasgow School of Art contemporary Margot Sandeman, in which she detailed: 'I think I will have to be very strong to stand against Mr. Cowie',[36] as well as Eardley's letter to her mother describing how, after being fairly quiet, she 'gave Mr. Cowie a piece of my mind'.[37] Despite the force of Cowie's artistic inclinations and the fact they diverged from Eardley's, her

FIG. 3.13

Nita Begg, Still Life, *1947*

oil on canvas, 31.8 x 33 cm / private collection, Scotland / © the artist's estate, all rights reserved

FIG. 3.14

Charles Pulsford, Untitled (Surrealist Townscape), *1939*

oil on plywood, 68.4 x 104.9 cm / National Galleries of Scotland, Edinburgh (presented by the artist's family, 2012)
© the artist's estate, all rights reserved / image courtesy of National Galleries of Scotland, 2017

acknowledgement that 'I know I am learning a lot in the way of painting from him',[38] and Cowie's respect for her work ethic,[39] a quality he encouraged and approved of in all his students, were paramount.

The degree and manner of influence Cowie had on the artistic development of the students who attended Hospitalfield during his Wardenship varied greatly. He was, at different times for different students, an authority figure to be overthrown, an irritant to be avoided, someone whose advice was respected despite differences in opinion, and an inspiring and formative guide. Regardless of the role he held for each individual, his leadership contributed to creating a learning environment of debate, dynamism and growth.

Hospitalfield during the Second World War

DAVID LOCKHART ON WARTIME AT HOSPITALFIELD

David Lockhart, RSW (1922–2014), came to Hospitalfield in 1944 as a student from Edinburgh College of Art along with friend and contemporary William McLaren (1923–1987). Wartime shaped their Hospitalfield experience:

'The war was on at the time – in fact, a very exciting part of the war. We were in the early weeks of the invasion of France, so we had a big map on the wall in the dining room and that was examined every night for the progress. It was an interesting regime at the College. The students did all the housework, all the sweeping, pre-Hoover days, brush and pan, all the carpeting, up and down the stairs and we worked until dinnertime and we were released after dinner just to go and paint.'[40]

The freedom of this time to paint proved a seminal experience for Lockhart. While surveying the many colourful paintings that hung on the walls of his home (where the interview that yielded these quotes was conducted in 2014), Lockhart concluded:

'This house has paintings everywhere and every brushstroke is due to Hospitalfield. I literally would never have developed as a painter without Hospitalfield. Hospitalfield not only made me realise I was a painter, it made me realise that I'd done the wrong thing at college, that I wasn't an illustrator.'[41]

Lockhart and McLaren remained lifelong friends and creative practitioners. The details of McLaren's exciting and varied career were captured in Jim Hickey's 2009 documentary film William McLaren: An Artist Out of Time. *Lockhart, as a member of the Royal Scottish Society of Painters in Watercolours and Head of the art department at Ballingry Junior High School developed as both a painter and a teacher. In 2012, he returned to Hospitalfield for a residency supported by the Hospitalfield Alumni Association.*[42]

Just as Hospitalfield felt the effects of the First World War, the Second World War also impacted the life of its residents. In 1939, unexpected events interrupted the students' residency as:

> The Government Evacuation Scheme brought to Hospitalfield, at two hours notice, twenty-one evacuees including five mothers. The urgency of the situation, the need of every available sleeping space, the uncertainty of our rights on the matter, compelled me to send our resident students home … the evacuees returned to their homes within a week and the students who had been sent away because of them came back and continued their work till the end of the session.[43]

Daily life was also affected because available staff for the house were in short supply. Cowie's 1945 report to the Trustees described: 'Our difficulties in the house, however, have been greater this year than in any since the War began – owing to the illness of Mrs. Cowie and the impossibility of finding a cook … our case was desperate indeed.'[44] The impact of the Second World War upon those at Hospitalfield was also recalled by Ruth Christie, Cowie's daughter, who described how 'students and household were all huddled in the Hospitalfield cellars in apprehension of bombs dropping on the nearby airfield.'[45]

The most significant change at Hospitalfield caused by the Second World War was the introduction of female students. The meeting minutes that recorded this change of policy did not explain the rationale.[46] It is likely that with enlistment already reducing art school enrolment, there were even fewer male students able to attend Hospitalfield. Just as women stepped into roles held by men in other areas of society, so too could female art students now take their place at Hospitalfield. Among these were Isabel Brodie Babianska, Marie de Banzie, Joan Eardley, Bet Low and many more who went on to contribute to the development of art in Scotland.[47] This change in policy set a precedent that continued to be applied at Hospitalfield throughout the rest of the twentieth century.

The Second World War was a fundamental part of the lives of a generation of young people who attended Hospitalfield under James Cowie and his successor Ian Fleming, RSA, RSW, RWA (1906–1994), and its effects were still felt in the post-war era. This is evident from an increase in the average age of those attending Hospitalfield and the appearance of students' war service records alongside their art-educational experiences in the Trustees' lists of admitted students. Rationing had been a daily reminder of wartime for all in Britain, including those at Hospitalfield. Despite continued rationing following the War, the specially prepared meals brought up on the dumb waiter and eaten in Hospitalfield's formal dining room seemed a sumptuous treat after wartime austerity and this left a distinct impression on many post-war students. While Hospitalfield's furnishings still retained a sense of the estate's former wealth and grandeur, its finances following the Second World War were, once again, ebbing. In an attempt to reduce expenditure, the length of the students' residencies was reduced from six months to three months.[48]

Warden Ian Fleming:
his work 1948–54

The painter, printmaker and teacher Ian Fleming became Warden when James Cowie moved to Edinburgh in 1948 as the newly elected Secretary of the Royal Scottish Academy. Many points of continuity carried through this transition of leadership. Fleming's artwork, like Cowie's, displayed a skilled handling of line and strength of composition. While informed by the visual world around him, it also reflected his knowledge of the Old Masters and of contemporary artistic idioms. These skills and practices not only became evident in the body of work Fleming developed at Hospitalfield, but also within the work of many of the students who came under his aegis.

The most significant difference between Cowie's and Fleming's approaches was the subject of their work and, in turn, the subject with which they encouraged the students to engage. Cowie's emphasis had been on composition pieces that combined still-life objects, figures and the landscape. Fleming focused on the landscape in its own right. Landscape painting had been a distinguishing feature of the curriculum of the Allan-Fraser Art College and a facet of the student experience under Cowie. Fleming's leadership, however, brought a renewed focus to the way Hospitalfield offered an opportunity for students to engage with the landscape.

Prior to becoming Warden of Hospitalfield, Fleming and his friend and contemporary William Wilson periodically travelled throughout Scotland to paint the landscape, but it was not until Fleming's time in Arbroath that he began to paint the coastline in earnest, developing a particular fascination with the harbour. The more time Fleming spent observing the visual environment of Arbroath and engaging with its community, the more he found to explore through his artwork. For example, a process of distilling the harbour into its essential forms can be seen by comparing his 1949 *Fisher Houses, Arbroath* (fig. 3.16), 1952 *Arbroath Harbour* (fig. 3.17) and 1952 *Harbour Pattern* (fig. 3.18). In *Fisher Houses*, the buildings project towards the viewer, asserting the illusion of three-dimensionality. Details of the buildings are then reduced in *Arbroath Harbour* to increase the emphasis upon their underlying geometric

HUGH ROBERTSON'S POST-WAR HOSPITALFIELD

Hugh Robertson (b.1922) trained at Glasgow School of Art. When the Second World War began he volunteered for fire-watching in the School, but like many of his contemporaries, was then called up to military service:

'I was in North Africa in '42. It was a very wild crossing. Very, very heavy seas. We were attacked by U-boats and spent the night just sitting below deck. The boat was swerving and you could hear the sounds of what was going on below. The boat beside us was hit with the Nazis on it. It was sunk. Once we got into the Mediterranean, it was flat calm. It took us almost a fortnight to go from the Clyde to Algiers. After that, I was in Tunisia and Italy. So that would have been three years.

'But because of my age, after the War finished, I still had a year to do. That's when I went to Florence and that was great, that was super. It was supposed to be for people interested in art or music. I got to know one of the instructors from the Royal College of Art and he became friendly with a chap who worked in the Uffizi Galleries, involved in the restorations of stuff that had been damaged during the war. You could travel all over the place.

'I was desperate to get back. At Hospitalfield Ian Fleming wasn't really doing any teaching, just advising, coming out to see what we were doing. The studio wasn't set up with a life class or anything, just encouraged to do our own thing. But having found a bicycle, Bill [Burns] and I were out on the bike tearing about the countryside, sketching and the like.'[49]

After attending Hospitalfield in 1949, Robertson began his career as an art teacher on the west coast of Scotland, a vocation that would last over thirty years.

ROBERT HENDERSON BLYTH

Robert Henderson Blyth, RSA, RSW (1919–1970), was educated at Glasgow School of Art and first attended Hospitalfield in 1938. During the Second World War, he served in the Royal Army Medical Corps in the European campaign and, afterwards, returned to Hospitalfield in 1946 on Cowie's invitation. Cowie was a formative influence for Henderson Blyth. At Hospitalfield, he, like Cowie, created compositions responding to his surroundings: the rural landscape, the sea, the still-life objects of the studio and his fellow art students. When his daily life and environment drastically changed on joining the Royal Army Medical Corps, so too did the imagery of his artwork. Although not an official War Artist, Henderson Blyth continued to draw, paint and exhibit his work throughout the War. Images he produced during and immediately after the War combined the clarity and complex compositions characteristic of Cowie's work with poignant, emotionally charged imagery. The battle-worn soldiers, the disenchanted youths and the war-torn landscapes — in paintings such as his 1942 Dispatch Rider, *1945* War Baby, 1918, *1946* Self-portrait as a Soldier in the Trenches: Existence Precarious *and 1947* In the Image of Man *— evoke raw emotion in their lamentation and consideration of the cost of war in terms of the loss of life, humanity and culture.*[50]

IAN FLEMING AND THE SECOND WORLD WAR

At the beginning of the Second World War, Fleming served as a Police War Reservist with the Maryhill Division in Glasgow because his position at Glasgow School of Art was an occupation classed as a 'reserve' that prevented him from enlisting. The etchings he created in response to the atmosphere of wartime Glasgow, particularly the devastation caused by the Clydebank bombing of 1941, form a poignant body of work. As the War progressed, Fleming was able to join the Pioneer Corps, supporting the frontline as it moved through France, Holland and Germany. Throughout this period, he continued to record his experiences and observations in drawings and paintings.[51]

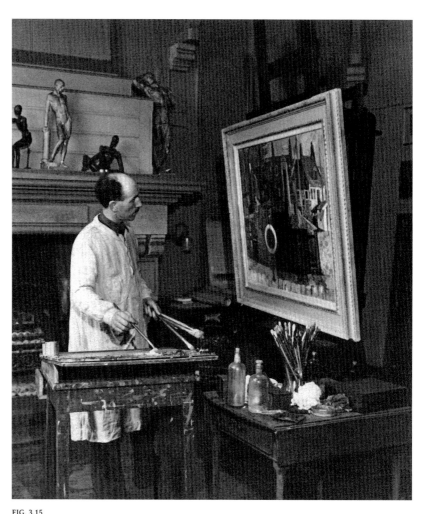

FIG. 3.15

Ian Fleming in the Hospitalfield Studio painting Fisher Houses, Arbroath

private collection, Scotland / image courtesy of Scottish Field and the artist's estate

FIG. 3.16

Ian Fleming, Fisher Houses, Arbroath, *1949*

structures. The sense of depth is also challenged, as the extreme tilting of the pier in the foreground contradicts the perspective established in the midground. In addition, the life-belt and stand, which span the height of the image, further emphasise the surface and two-dimensionality of the image. This sense of two-dimensionality increases in *Harbour Pattern*, which reduces the harbour buildings, the harbour wall and the life-preservers to geometric patches of paint. These paintings are representative of Fleming's process of continuously reinterpreting the landscape through form and composition, a practice which would continue to develop during and following his time at Hospitalfield.

Although Fleming continually experimented with aspects of abstraction, reaching a non-representational image was not his ultimate aim. Rather, the connection between image and place was of the utmost importance. Fleming's work was informed by his link to the community in which he lived and worked. So while he was Warden of Hospitalfield, he not only painted the Arbroath landscape, he also became a part of the town's cultural life. As Chairman of the Arbroath Art Society and a Rotarian, he sought to be an ambassador for art, frequently giving public lectures. These encouraged the public to become

FIG. 3.17

Ian Fleming, Arbroath Harbour, *1952*

oil on canvas, 59 x 89 cm / Angus Council Collections managed by ANGUSalive Museums, Galleries & Archives
(gift from Arbroath Art Society and Arbroath Town Improvement Trust, 1955)
© the artist's estate, all rights reserved / image courtesy of Angus Council, 2017

FIG. 3.18

Ian Fleming, Harbour Pattern, *1952*

oil on board, 79 x 44 cm / The Hunterian, University of Glasgow, Glasgow (Scottish Arts Council Collection bequest, 1997)

IAN FLEMING ON ART

Ian Fleming valued artistic skill, knowledge exchange across media, an institutional co-operative spirit, and the cultural importance of art. His ethos about art and education lives on through his students and his legacy at Gray's School of Art and Peacock Printmakers in Aberdeen. Here are some of his words:

'I was always fascinated by a sharp point, I like a line ... you've got to be absolutely precise and know that line goes from there to there.'[52]

'I always regarded Art as being an expression of the individual and his emotional reaction to the visual world.'[53]

'I had always felt the need to express some social comment in my subject matter.'[54]

familiar with the work of painters in their own community, broaden their understanding of modern art and consider the visual world around them in a different way.

Enabling the viewing public to engage with his and his contemporaries' paintings of familiar places was also an important facet of his practice. To this effect, he stated in a speech he made at the opening of the 1948 Arbroath Art Society exhibition:

> If you look at this interpretation of your neighbourhood ... do not readily condemn them if you do not think they are correct. Rather ask yourself and say 'Perhaps I am wrong. Perhaps I am not sensitive of the beauty of line, form and colour.' If you have time go again and look at the places portrayed by the artists and see if you can enlarge your experience by seeing them through his eyes. You will then be able to appreciate art more fully.[55]

The composition of many of Fleming's Arbroath landscapes orientated the viewer in a way that promoted their direct engagement with the image. For instance, the high skyline and large foreground of his 1949 *Fisher Houses* or 1952 *Arbroath Harbour* situates the viewer as if they were standing on the rocky shoreline below the pier. Paintings like these thereby encourage the viewer not only to see, but also to experience, the sense of place as interpreted by Fleming.

Achieving this type of experiential quality through composition had historical precedents of which Fleming would have been aware. The painting *St John Preaching in the Wilderness*, date unknown (fig. 3.19), by Pieter Brueghel the Younger,[56] which hung in Arbroath Library, also used composition to position the viewer to 'enter' the foreground. As Brueghel was a particular favourite of Fleming's,[57] he surely studied these locally available paintings. Furthermore, because Brueghel's time and place was significant to his work,[58] it would have provided a relevant point of reference as Fleming sought to interpret the life and landscape of Arbroath. Fleming, a native of Glasgow, would also have been familiar with the work of the Glasgow Boys, whose paintings frequently featured the type of composition that engendered an immersive experience.[59] For instance, James Guthrie's 1883 *A Hind's Daughter* (fig. 3.20) employs a high skyline and large forward-tipping foreground that places the viewer at a vantage point within the field.

There were not only compositional similarities between works like Guthrie's *A Hind's Daughter* and Fleming's Arbroath paintings, but also comparable conceptual approaches. Just as Guthrie informed his paintings through his knowledge of the life and landscape of Cocksburnpath,[60] where he chose to live and work, so too did Fleming. The title of his 1949 painting *Danger Point* indicated that this setting was not of an anonymous generic harbour scene. Instead, the image depicted the oldest part of the Arbroath harbour established in 1394 by Abbot John Gedy, which was later named after the number of shipwrecks that occurred off the coast. Through the menacing sky and waving nets in *Danger Point*, Fleming alluded to the site's history. With Arbroath still heavily reliant on the fishing industry at this time, this painting also conveyed the precarious, but essential, relationship between the sea and the community.

While there are echoes of the nineteenth-century Scottish artistic tradition in Fleming's paintings and practice, there are also traces of nineteenth-century French artistic aesthetics and ideologies because of the historic connection between Scotland and France and the centuries of exchange between their artists. The 'immersive' composition used by Guthrie and, later, Fleming

FIG. 3.19

Pieter Brueghel the Younger, St John Preaching in the Wilderness

oil on board, 105 x 150 cm / Angus Council Collections managed by ANGUSalive Museums, Galleries & Archives (gift from James Renny, 1876) / image courtesy of Angus Council, 2017

FIG. 3.20

Sir James Guthrie, A Hind's Daughter, *1883*

oil on canvas, 91.5 x 76.2 cm / National Galleries of Scotland, Edinburgh (bequest of Sir James Lewis Caw, 1951)
image courtesy of National Galleries of Scotland, 2017

was similarly employed by Jules Bastien-Lepage.[61] Furthermore, Fleming's devotion to painting the landscape of the community in which he lived was reminiscent of the belief espoused by French landscape painter Georges Michel (1763–1843) that 'the man who cannot paint for a lifetime within an area of ten miles is just a clumsy fool who ... will find nothing but emptiness.'[62] Fleming's reinvention of this practice within a new context exemplified the continued interconnection between the Scottish and French painting traditions.

While his practice had historic connections, it also had contemporary relevance. Books such as Herbert Read's 1937 *Art and Society* and Arnold Hauser's 1951 *The Social History of Art*, which explored the social function of art, marked an increasing interest in this concept among the artistic community of the United Kingdom. These ideologies became particularly relevant for Fleming as well as for artists such as James McIntosh Patrick, Joan Eardley and James Morrison. Although working in different aesthetics, each was equally committed to painting the landscape and communities in which they lived on the northeast coast of Scotland. The following chapter will discuss how McIntosh Patrick, Eardley and Morrison, as artists in residence, would continue the legacy Fleming established at Hospitalfield. It will also further explore the way in which these artists contributed to the formation of a northeastern culture of landscape painting.

When Fleming moved to Aberdeen in 1954, the practice and coastal imagery he developed during his time in Arbroath continued to evolve. Works such as his 1964 *Gourdon Dusk*, *c.*1969 *Harbour Morning* and 1987 *Harbour Pattern: The Rainbow* exemplify his reinvention and reinvestigation of the visual environment in his locale. Being Warden of Hospitalfield was therefore significant to his artistic evolution. It allowed him the time, facilities and opportunity to experiment with aesthetics and clarify the conceptual approach that would direct his work for the rest of his career. It also enabled him to share his practice with the students, many of whom would develop their own practices in relation to the landscape.

Warden Ian Fleming: his influence 1948–54

In his 1948 report to the Trustees, Fleming explained:

> I laid down as principle that the work done at Hospitalfield should be out of doors. I feel that the students have all had experience and the opportunity to develop the more indoor side of an artist's training, namely portraits, still-life, and figure.[63]

Fleming's statement reveals that, from the beginning of his time as Warden, he established that the Scheme's priority would be to encourage landscape painting. This both augmented the curricula of the Scottish art colleges and aligned with Fleming's own practice.

The effect of this emphasis as well as Fleming's particular influence are evident in the work of William Burns, RSA, RSW (1921–1972). Burns first attended Hospitalfield in 1948 from Glasgow School of Art and quickly acclimatised to painting his surroundings in Arbroath. A review of the exhibition of Hospitalfield students' work from that summer in *The Arbroath Herald* proclaimed: 'Burns' work has a sensitivity of colour treatment that has captured the intrinsic quality of the scenes and buildings he has sought to depict.'[64] The subtle tonal shifts in subsequent paintings by Burns that bring to life the textures and atmosphere of the harbour environment, such as his 1952–5 *Nets*, exemplify the effect to which the review referred. The influence of this experience is also evident from Burns' continued engagement with coastal imagery. As a student, he returned to Arbroath under the Scheme in 1949 and continued to frequent Hospitalfield throughout the 1950s as a family friend of the Flemings.

During this period, many parallels existed between Fleming's and Burns' paintings. Not only did both artists seek comparable subjects at the Arbroath harbour and in Scotland's coastal towns, but both valued similar stylistic qualities. For example, both Burns and Fleming used a tonal palette to explore the effects of light and shadow and emphasise structure and form. The understanding and exchange between these two artists is further evident in Fleming's portrait of Burns (fig. 3.21). In this painting, Burns is depicted at work, paintbrush in hand. Over his right shoulder is a view of Arbroath. Due to the ambiguity of perspective as well as the stylistic qualities shared by Fleming and Burns, it is impossible to determine if Fleming has painted the view to the harbour as he would represent it or if this is a painting by Burns that leans against the wall. Either way, it serves as a record of Fleming and Burns' association at Hospitalfield and the importance that the surrounding landscape had within their work.

When Burns became a lecturer at Aberdeen College of Education in 1955, he settled 45 miles north of Arbroath in the fishing village of Portlethen. Although the coastal environment continued to inspire his work, the aesthetic through which he interpreted the landscape shifted from representation to

FIG. 3.21

Ian Fleming, William A. Burns, *1950–4*

oil on canvas mounted on board, 101 x 76 cm / Aberdeen Art Gallery & Museums Collections, Aberdeen (purchased 1981)
© the artist's estate, all rights reserved / image courtesy of Aberdeen Art Gallery & Museums, 2017

abstraction. The type of organic forms that composed the rocky shores of his coastal paintings of the 1950s increasingly appeared on a larger scale as he distilled the shoreline into textural patches of colour. These colours also evolved from subtle tonality to bold rich reds. Like the English painter Peter Lanyon, Burns' passion for flying informed his work, with many of his paintings capturing the essence of the landscape as viewed from above. Tragically, his inspiration also led to his death when his plane went down during a solo flight in 1972.[65] Although his career was cut short, Burns' legacy is preserved in his dynamic evocations of the northeastern coast, images whose origins can be traced to his time at Hospitalfield.

The opportunity to engage with the landscape had a significant influence upon the artistic development of Frances Walker, who attended Hospitalfield in 1952 as a student from Edinburgh College of Art.[66] An immediate impact of the experience of working directly in the landscape can be seen in the stylistic qualities of Walker's paintings from that summer. For instance, the vibrant greens in her *Summer Hayfield* (fig. 3.22) reflect her observation of the colours of the landscape illuminated by the summer sun, while the loose brushstrokes used to create the texture of the upturned soil in *Empty Potato Field* (fig. 3.23) exemplify how working *en plein air* inspired her to work with greater immediacy. A comparison of *Summer Hayfield* and *Empty Potato Field* also reveals Walker's process of observing and responding to the changing colour of, and activity in, the landscape as it shifted from the rich greens and yellows of the early summer season of growth to the brown and red exposed soil of the late summer harvest. In addition, these paintings capture a more ephemeral atmospheric change. *Summer Hayfield*, with its landscape of vitality and reclining youth, whose repose embodies an attitude of dreamy wistfulness, conveys a sense of hope and promise. In contrast, the abandoned baskets in *Empty Potato Field* have the poignant revelry of a season's end.

The way *Summer Hayfield* and *Empty Potato Field* express the changing character of the season was informed by Walker's own experience with the land. Having grown up in a house that belonged to the Raith Estate on one of their farms outside Kirkcaldy, she was intimately familiar with agricultural ways of life. Her experience and connection with the land expanded as she joined the National Union of Students work camps in the summers between academic sessions at Edinburgh College of Art to bring in the harvest, be it picking strawberries in Wisbech, Cambridgeshire, peas in Lancashire, working in the bramble lanes of Norfolk or the corn, wheat, and barley fields of Caithness and Perthshire. As these points of reference informed her work, *Summer Hayfield* and *Empty Potato Field* are more than just pastoral scenes. They have a distinct authenticity of viewpoint that communicates the vital importance of agriculture and the harvest in providing food for the population during the immediate post-war years.[67]

Although the aesthetic of Walker's later work is more linear and less painterly than that of her student paintings, her process of observing, connecting with and responding to the land, which began to develop at Hospitalfield, continued to inform her practice throughout her career. This is particularly evident in those landscapes that captured the Aberdeen shoreline and landscape of Tiree, places that were both Walker's artistic subject and her home. Furthermore, Walker's practice continues to involve responding to a sense of place. In her contemporary work, as in *Summer Hayfield* and *Empty Potato Field*, the visual qualities of the landscape and the presence of a community and its evolving relationship with the land are considered and interpreted.

FIG. 3.22

Frances Walker, Summer Hayfield, *1952*

SUMMER HAYFIELD

The figure in Summer Hayfield *was based upon Walker's friend — and Edinburgh College of Art and Hospitalfield contemporary — Ella McCalman (née Leslie). After Hospitalfield, McCalman and Walker remained close friends, making an artistic journey across Europe a few years later. Eventually settling on Islay, McCalman devoted many years to teaching art. In 2002, McCalman's former student, Raymond Lafferty, spent several months at Hospitalfield through a residency awarded by the Royal Scottish Academy. Lafferty used this opportunity to create landscape and figure drawings in charcoal and conté crayon for an exhibition at the Rendezvous Gallery in Aberdeen. This interweaving of the Hospitalfield experience exemplifies its multi-generational connections and impact.*

FRANCES WALKER RECOUNTS PAINTING THE LANDSCAPE

'It was haymaking when I first came and then the corn and then finally it was the tattie howking. I had never worked outside in that way before. I'd been at art college in the centre of Edinburgh and the stuff I'd been doing was dark. So the fantastic thing that happened was the tone of my paintings just shot up. We went on the old bikes that were there for us to use, off to St Vigeans or further afield, went down to the harbour, painted and drew down there. Leaving your painting inside a stook and going back for it the next day — nobody seemed to bother or take it. We did a lot of work; we were constantly, every day out doing something. And then there were the studios, lovely big lofty spaces, which we basically tended to use on the duller and wet days or to finish something off. I know that possibly in later years people did more studio work, but I don't know what it was, I not only wanted to be outdoors, but it was such a refreshing change from working indoors in Edinburgh College of Art and there's no question that the tone of my painting went up.'[68]

Throughout her career Frances Walker (b.1930), RSA, RSW, D.Litt, Honorary Fellow of Edinburgh College of Art, has continuously interpreted northern landscapes where sea, land and sky meet and has influenced generations of students through her teaching.

FIG. 3.23

Frances Walker, Empty Potato Field, *1952*

oil on board, 50.8 x 76.2 cm / University of Edinburgh Art Collection, Edinburgh: EU3249
(retained from student work done at Hospitalfield Art College)
© Frances Walker, all rights reserved / image courtesy of Edinburgh University, 2017

FIG. 3.24

Morris Grassie, The Sou'Wester, Arbroath, c.*1957*

oil on gesso board, 76.2 x 101.6 cm / City Art Centre, Museum & Galleries Edinburgh / © Morris Grassie, all rights reserved / image © Antonia Reeve, courtesy of City Art Centre, 2017

While Walker could relate to the countryside surrounding Hospitalfield, her fellow 1952 Hospitalfield student Morris Grassie, as a native of Arbroath, had an even more intimate understanding. As previously mentioned, Grassie frequented Hospitalfield under James Cowie as a young art student in Arbroath. Grassie's work from his time as a residential student in 1952 and 1953, like that of Burns and Walker, reflected his engagement with the landscape. His harbour triptych, in particular – one part of which is illustrated here (fig. 3.24) – reflects both Fleming's direct influence and his personal connection to Arbroath.

Seeing that Grassie had collected numerous studies of the harbour, Fleming suggested that he use them to construct a triptych of compositions. The setting of the triptych aligned with Fleming's frequent use of harbour imagery. Furthermore, Grassie used a high skyline and large foreground to create the immersive effect characteristic of many of Fleming's paintings.

As the harbour views in the triptych were composite images formed from numerous studies, rather than a singularly observed scene, Grassie took the opportunity to include a reference to his family's connection to the harbour by featuring his grandmother's house in the background. While Fleming's harbour scenes suggest the community, but do not emphasise figuration, people are central to Grassie's triptych. In the central panel are fishermen engaged in their daily activities. Yet these are not anonymous figures, but based upon studies of his uncles. This reinforces how Grassie's painting was informed by his first-hand experience and familial connection to the harbour. That his uncle, Thomas Adams, on which the rightmost figure was based, later died in a lifeboat accident off the coast of Arbroath, adds poignancy to the image. In this way, the meaning of the painting evolved to convey the risk that generations of fishermen accepted as a necessary part of their livelihood.[69]

While Grassie's paintings are reflective of his family history as well as his engagement with Fleming at Hospitalfield, they also relate to trends in English painting. Beginning in the 1920s with artists like Christopher Wood and continuing into the 1950s with the work of painters like Prunella Clough, landscape evolved as a medium for expressing emotion and exploring concepts of identity. With travel restricted during and after the Second World War, many British artists looked to their surroundings and their artistic heritage as points of reference and inspiration. Using various idioms of representation and abstraction and differing conceptual approaches, artists including Graham Sutherland, Paul Nash, John Craxton, John Minton, John Piper and Keith Vaughan reinvented the British landscape tradition.[70] While diverse in their artistic affinities, it was their collective interest in interpreting a sense of place that related to the culture of imagery that was evolving and would continue to evolve at Hospitalfield.

Aside from offering an opportunity to seek inspiration from the landscape, the Scheme as directed by Fleming also provided a chance for students from the four Scottish art colleges to learn from one another. Believing that 'the interchange of ideas and influences from the different colleges is one of the best features of a college like Hospitalfield',[71] Fleming encouraged an atmosphere of conversation and exchange.

Grassie's 1952 self-portrait (fig. 3.25) exemplifies the type of result this atmosphere could produce. Although Grassie had planned to paint a self-portrait, it was his new-found friend Archie Graham, from Glasgow School of Art, who inspired him to do so by applying paint with a palette knife rather than painting with a brush. The opportunity to experiment with this technique used at Glasgow, but not at Dundee, enabled Grassie to gain a new perspective about the relationship between painting method and aesthetic emphasis, thereby concentrating 'much more on the design with the palette

FIG. 3.25

Morris Grassie, Self Portrait in the Four Poster Bed at Hospitalfield, *1952*

oil on canvas, 63 x 75 cm / private collection, Scotland / © Morris Grassie, all rights reserved / image courtesy of Andrew Grassie, 2017

knife, rather than the freedom of a brush, which is more expressive'.[72]

The vibrancy of the thick paint, whose colours were intensified through their contrast, gives this work a sumptuous and dynamic quality. The richness of the pigments and patterns of Grassie's self-portrait were reminiscent of the paintings of nineteenth-century French artists Pierre Bonnard and Édouard Vuillard. This evocation is another example of the continuation of the historic artistic connection between Scotland and France. Being among the Post-Impressionists, Bonnard and Vuillard, of course, preceded Grassie. Their revolutionary use of colour contributed to the multitude of artistic innovations generated at the end of the nineteenth and beginning of the twentieth century, during which time the Glasgow Boys, the Glasgow Style and the Scottish Colourists also emerged. As this period produced so many new ideas about art, many British painters, even by the 1950s, were still testing techniques and concepts introduced fifty years previously.[73] It was at Hospitalfield, offering a space outside the structured curriculum of the Scottish art colleges, that students could engage in such experimentation. As L.J.A. Bell characterised in his 1954 *Scotland's Magazine* article 'Scotland's Smallest Art School', at Hospitalfield 'selected students may work all the summer through; sharing their meals, sharing their ideas with students from other colleges, getting away from the artistic gods on which they have been leaning through all the years of study'.[74]

In the coming years, with the art colleges' curricula remaining regimented skills-based programmes, the avant-garde progressing ever forward, and new innovations in art coming into Scotland as the United Kingdom was once more engaged in international exchange, the opportunity for knowledge sharing and experimentation that Hospitalfield provided became increasingly significant. This aspect of the Hospitalfield experience would, however, develop under a new regime. When Fleming departed Hospitalfield in 1954 to become Principal of Gray's School of Art in Aberdeen, a new dynamic of leadership was introduced. While this ended the succession of Artist-Wardens, the bodies of work Cowie and Fleming produced at Hospitalfield created a lasting legacy within Scottish painting. Such was the significance of this work to the art of Scotland that L.J.A. Bell concluded: 'if Hospitalfield did no more than provide for artists like Cowie and Fleming to produce art, it is worthwhile.'[75] Their contributions to Scottish art also extended to the opportunities that their leadership of Hospitalfield's programme offered the students. Under Cowie and Fleming, students from the four Scottish art colleges encountered not only the new artistic influences of the Warden, but also that of their peers. In addition, they were able to engage with the local landscape and begin to cultivate their own practices. It would be these aspects of the student experience that would continue to impact the development of the young artists who attended Hospitalfield throughout the rest of the twentieth century.

4

Artistic innovation, experimentation and exchange
The Patrick Allan-Fraser Trust Scheme 1954–70

The harbour paintings Ian Fleming created during his time as Warden and Fleming's continued fascination with coastal imagery proved influential for many students who attended Gray's School of Art, Aberdeen, during his time as Principal (1954–72). This was true for Will Maclean, who frequently found subjects for his work at the harbour during his summer at Hospitalfield. Smokies Sold Here *exemplifies Maclean's exploration of the surfaces and colours of the harbour as well as his ability to connect to a sense of place, for although this landscape is uninhabited, the presence of its community is suggested through the clothes on the line, the fishing nets and the smoking house. While Maclean's style would evolve away from a type of semi-abstract tonal painting akin to Fleming's, his intense observation of, and sensitivity towards, the landscape, evident in this painting, would prove significant in his later explorations of the personal and cultural meaning of subjects such as the Scottish fishing industry and the Highland Clearances.*

Although situated outside the town centre of Arbroath, Hospitalfield had always been an intrinsic part of the community. Patrick Allan-Fraser was a civically active individual who believed in supporting the community, particularly local craftsmen.[1] After his death in 1890, Hospitalfield House not only became the site of the Allan-Fraser Art College, but was also opened to visitors during the summer.[2] While members of the community occasionally questioned if the College did enough to cultivate local talent in the spirit of its founder,[3] ultimately, the Arbroath Provost's vehement support for the College's preservation demonstrated its significance to the town's economic and cultural life. When the Patrick Allan-Fraser Trust Scheme replaced the College, its Wardens maintained the tradition of admitting the public during the summer. In addition, James Cowie and Ian Fleming strengthened bonds between Hospitalfield and Arbroath through their involvement in the Arbroath Art Society.[4] The appointment of William Reid (1909–1973) as Fleming's successor in 1954 only increased this connection.

Reid began his artistic career at Dundee College of Art, achieving his Diploma in Design and Decorative Arts in 1930 and a Post-Diploma in Design in 1931. On returning from a travelling scholarship, he began teaching art in Dundee and Angus schools. After serving in the Royal Air Force during the Second World War, he was appointed Head of the art department at Arbroath High School and, along with Cowie, became a founder member of the revived Arbroath Art Society in 1946. For Reid, like the Allan-Fraser Art College's Governor Peter Munnoch, teaching art became his passion and life's work. Reid's enthusiasm fostered an active art department at Arbroath High School, whose staff included former Hospitalfield participants William Littlejohn and Joan Cuthill.[5] With students from the four Scottish art colleges resident at Hospitalfield only during the summer months, his duties as Warden[6] and his job as a teacher could be complementary. It was therefore agreed between Reid and the Trustees that his chief priorities as Warden would be the management of Hospitalfield House and the pastoral care of the students.

During Fleming's Wardenship, William Burns and Joan Eardley had been artists in residence in an informal capacity, working for periods at Hospitalfield in 1952 and 1953 and interacting with the students during this time. Under Reid, having an artist in residence who could work at Hospitalfield and provide the students with guidance and support became a formalised annual occurrence.[7] With authority now split between Reid and the artists in residence, greater autonomy, exchange and experimentation prevailed among the students of this era.

The way in which Hospitalfield's learning environment cultivated artistic experimentation and independence is exemplified by the experiences of 1965 Hospitalfield students George Donald (b.1943), RSA, RSW, and Will Maclean (b.1941), D.Litt., RSA, RSW, RGI, MBE. Upon discovering a derelict etching

FIG. 4.1

Will Maclean, Smokies Sold Here, *1965*

oil on board, 90 x 56 cm / private collection, Scotland / © Will Maclean, all rights reserved / image courtesy of the artist, 2017

ARTISTIC INNOVATION, EXPERIMENTATION AND EXCHANGE 81

FIG. 4.2

Joyce W. Cairns, Girl in the Landscape, *1969*

acrylic on canvas, 97 x 81 cm / property of the artist / © Joyce W. Cairns, all rights reserved / image courtesy of the artist, 2017

press[8] in one of Hospitalfield's outbuildings, Maclean, Donald and their fellow students took it upon themselves to restore the press and experiment in printmaking; something they had limited opportunities to pursue within the confines of their education in drawing and painting. When recalling this time at Hospitalfield, Donald described the way serendipitous circumstances led to new creative possibilities.[9] While seeking a new part for the press at an engineering works in Arbroath, he discovered scrap copper sheets, which he then used as his printing plates. This concept inspired several series of prints in which differently shaped plates were combined and reconfigured into jigsaw-like patterns to produce varying visual emphases. The continued legacy of this experience has been evident throughout Donald's and Maclean's careers, as printmaking has remained a part of their practices.

Maclean's and Donald's experiences at Hospitalfield also had more ephemeral impacts upon their artistic development. Maclean reflected that Hospitalfield's 'different kind of learning experience, which came from the freedom that you got there, provided confidence and assurance'.[10] For Donald, Hospitalfield proved a seminal and transformative experience: 'I came as a student, but left with the commitment to be an artist, with all the ways of thinking, being and doing that brings.'[11]

By offering a time for creative ventures beyond the art colleges' structured curricula, the Patrick Allan-Fraser Trust Scheme was beneficial for young artists because of the freedom of artistic experimentation it allowed. Such was the case for Joyce W. Cairns (b.1947), RSA, RSW, Hon. RBA, MA (RCA), a Gray's School of Art student who was at Hospitalfield in 1969.[12] Her time there was one of artistic exploration, during which she created a variety of work ranging from studies of the coastal landscape and abstract configurations of colours and patterns to compositions combining the observed and the imagined, as exemplified by her 1969 Hospitalfield painting *Girl in the Landscape* (fig. 4.2).[13]

This body of work became a reservoir from which to draw when Cairns returned to Gray's for her final Diploma year, after which she was awarded a Post-Diploma year of study. As Cairns continued her development as a painter through a Master of Arts at the Royal College of Art, was awarded a year's Fellowship at Gloucestershire College of Art and Design in Cheltenham, and completed the Art Teacher's Certificate course at Goldsmiths, University of London, the influence of the Hospitalfield experience was continually present.

The process of navigating the pictorial relationships between figures, animals, aspects of landscapes, objects and design, which developed at Hospitalfield, also remained a significant aspect of painting throughout Cairns' career. Using the type of visual synthesis evident in *Girl in a Landscape*, both her early and contemporary work transports the viewer into painted worlds where figures, objects and patterns form evocative narratives.[14] Hindsight therefore reveals that the Scheme provided for Cairns, and many others, an essential developmental phase from which future practice could evolve.

Hospitalfield was the only joint venture between all four Scottish art colleges that enabled students to engage with one another for an extended period of time. By bringing together students who shared a commitment to art and an enthusiastic, youthful energy, the experience fostered a sense of community. This proved significant for individuals and for connecting otherwise disparate subsections of the Scottish art world. The importance of this effect was noted by the painter Jack Knox, who attended Hospitalfield as a student from Glasgow School of Art in 1957 and returned as an artist in residence in 1968. In his 1968 report to the Trustees, he emphasised how Hospitalfield's artistic community

... can open their minds to new ideas, simply by being in the company of other young painters who are also just discovering what art is all about. (This aspect of Hospitalfield, which one might call the social side, is as important as what goes on in the studios).[15]

What Knox observed among the students in 1968 reflected his own experience as a student. The friendship he formed that summer with Ian McKenzie Smith, attending from Gray's School of Art, started a chain of events that changed both of their artistic careers.

The exchange of ideas and techniques that often arose from the Hospitalfield students' sociability is seen, for example, in the experience of Jean Martin, RSW, who participated in the Patrick Allan-Fraser Trust Scheme in 1967 as a student from Glasgow School of Art. At that time, the drawing and painting departments of the four Scottish art colleges still shared similar

FIG. 4.3

Jean Martin, Fred the Gardener, *1967*

oil on canvas, 90 x 62 cm / private collection, Scotland
© Jean Martin, all rights reserved / image courtesy of the artist, 2017

curricular values, such as teaching students how to draw and paint from observation and structurally compose their images. The different artistic inclinations of each college and departmental staff members, however, meant that the style guidelines under which such work was created varied. For instance, the drawing and painting faculty at Glasgow School of Art, including Mary Armour, David Donaldson and Geoffrey Squire, taught students to paint with thick impasto in a gestural, expressive way. Being able to discover a different way of painting at Hospitalfield, by observing the work of Edinburgh College of Art students Gillian Mather[16] and Rosemary Hamblin, therefore, proved a revelation for Martin.

The subtle tonality and thinly applied oil paint that characterises Martin's 1967 portrait of Hospitalfield's head gardener, Fred (fig. 4.3), reveals a departure from increasing the thickness of paint as the painting developed, a process she had often found unsatisfying in its finished outcome. Instead, by utilising the technique of glazing, gradually layering translucent applications of paint as Hamblin and Mather did, Martin found a way of working that resonated with the type of subtle, but richly painted, surface she wanted to achieve. Upon returning to art school, Martin continued to explore the application of this style of painting, an exploration that continues to connect to the type of luminosity and layering seen in her contemporary work.[17]

The impact of the artists in residence

While the students learned from one another, they also had the opportunity to encounter the influences of the artists in residence. Initially, the Trustees wanted distinguished English painters to fill this role:

> having in mind the desirability of giving the course at Hospitalfield a distinctive character and of providing fresh interest, the Sub-Committee agreed … of obtaining a Guest Artist under whom the students were unlikely to have had the opportunity of studying previously.[19]

James Bateman (1893–1959), the first official artist in residence (appointed in 1955), matched these criteria. He had trained at Leeds School of Art, the Royal College of Art and the Slade, was the former painting master at Cheltenham School of Art and Hammersmith School of Art, and was a member of the Royal Academy. After Bateman, the Trustees were unable to attract another artist with similar qualifications. Whether other English artists declined due to the distance, insufficient compensation or the time of year of the residency is unknown, but this disinclination caused the Trustees to change their rationale. Instead, they invited artists in residence who lived and worked in Scotland. Drawing from a more local populace of painters did not equate to a provincial outlook. The Scotland-based artists invited for residencies were each producing individually innovative work and actively engaging with the mid-century culture of painting.

The wide range of artistic practices, experiences and outlooks of the artists in residence meant the influences introduced to the students were less consistent, but more varied, than when Cowie or Fleming were Warden. From these diverse influences, two trends emerged: landscape and abstract painting. The pervasiveness of students working *en plein air* and the invitation of artists in residence who engaged with landscape in their practices continued the precedent that Fleming had established. In addition, the increased interest in abstraction among the artists in residence and the students introduced a new aesthetic tendency to the Hospitalfield experience that would remain significant in the coming years.

IAN MCKENZIE SMITH ON A CHANCE ENCOUNTER WITH ABSTRACT EXPRESSIONISM

'Jack Knox got the travelling scholarship from Glasgow School of Art and I got the travelling scholarship from Gray's School of Art, Aberdeen. We decided we would jointly go to Paris to start off and we later went to Brussels by train. Purely by chance (and I'm saying this because we could have turned left or right going down this street) there was a rear doorway and it turned out to be an entrance to a great gallery. We were both absolutely stunned by this exhibition of American Abstract Expressionist painting. That was an exhibition that would stick in my mind. All the painters were there. It was the first we had heard of — never mind seen — the work of Jackson Pollock, [William] Baziotes, Barnett Newman. It was quite an eye opener.' [18]

For McKenzie Smith (b.1935), CBE, FRSA, FRSE, HRA, HRHA, PPRSA, PPRSW, LLD, RGI, *developing a personal language of abstraction remained central to his practice throughout his career and still occupies the focus of his contemporary work.*

The exhibition's influence on Knox (1936–2015), RSA, RGI, RSW, HFRIAS, *is most evident in his gestural abstract paintings of the 1960s. After this period, his use of abstraction became increasingly geometric, before he was inspired to return to a representational mode of working.*

Approaches to landscape

To the students of 1956, John Maclauchlan Milne brought an artistic perspective that reflected the 'auld alliance', the exchange between Scotland and France.[20] Born in 1885, Milne was trained by his father, Joseph Milne, and uncle, William Watt Milne. As a young artist, he spent periods living and working in Paris and the French countryside, returning intermittently to Scotland until he settled on Arran in the 1940s. His simplification of form in order to emphasise his use of vibrant colour was akin to contemporaries of his such as Samuel John Peploe, Francis Campbell Boileau Cadell and other artists now known as the Scottish Colourists. The saturation of tone in works like Maclauchlan Milne's *Harvest Field* (fig. 4.4) can be considered a response to, as well as a translation of, the landscape. This practice echoed the advice given to Paul Sérusier in 1888 at Pont Aven by Paul Gauguin, who, according to Maurice Denis, encouraged Sérusier to use the most saturated form of the colours he observed in the landscape when making a painting.[21] Bringing this type of knowledge and perspective to the students at Hospitalfield can be considered one of Maclauchlan Milne's last contributions to Scottish painting. Shortly after his summer at Hospitalfield his health declined and he died just over a year later.

For Ian McCulloch, the source material he gathered at the Arbroath harbour formed the inspiration for a ceramic plaque (fig. 4.5) that he created on his return to Glasgow School of Art. The plaque transforms the essence of the harbour, once captured in sketches, into a final work that combines painted two-dimensional and formed three-dimensional elements. In style, it is reminiscent of English neo-Romantic painters like John Minton and Christopher Wood. This plaque exemplifies how the fusion of Hospitalfield's stimulating visual environment, artistic influences and an artist's personal vision could result in the creation of unique works.

A more direct aesthetic legacy from Maclauchlan Milne's landscapes is evident in the work of 1960 artist in residence John Cunningham, RGI (1926–1998). Using intense colour and vigorous brushstrokes, Cunningham engaged with the visual language of the Colourists. His vibrant interpretations of the landscape demonstrate the continued importance of developments in late nineteenth and early twentieth-century French and Scottish painting within mid-twentieth-century Scottish art.

The landscape tradition in Scottish painting would be interpreted and expanded through a variety of aesthetics during the twentieth century. Another contributor to this genre was James McIntosh Patrick, RSA, ROI, ARE (1907–1998), who served as artist in residence from 1957 to 1959. Studying at Glasgow School of Art between 1924 and 1928, McIntosh Patrick first became known for the clarity, detail and strong compositional form of his paintings and etchings throughout the 1920s and 1930s. During the Second World War, he worked as a camouflage painter, but continued his practice when he had the opportunity. After experiencing the immediacy of response

IAN MCCULLOCH ON JOHN MACLAUCHLAN MILNE

For a 1938 exhibition catalogue, Maclauchlan Milne, RSA (1885–1957), wrote: 'Art is not a thing but a way, a way of apprehending reality.'[22] This statement provides insight into the philosophical underpinning behind Maclauchlan Milne's seemingly benign colourful landscapes. It also resonates with the subsequent response of Ian McCulloch, RSA, to the advice Maclauchlan Milne provided at Hospitalfield:

'The thing that always struck me, stuck in my mind, and still is influencing me, is that he said to the student, 'When you're painting that hillside, look at a melon, look at the colours in the melon and use and apply them to the hillside', which seemed a kind of, at that time, dishonest thing to say. But thinking about it, it seemed to me that what he was suggesting was something much more significant and profound. He was talking about how you could transpose one image or part of an image, which apparently had nothing to do with the thing you were working on; how you could take it and apparently, quite arbitrarily, implicate it into what you were doing. I still think about this when I'm in the studio now, and obviously what I'm doing is very different from anything that Maclauchlan Milne would have done, but what I'm realising is that I can take aspects of one drawing and one idea and take something which is quite different and based on a different drawing, and which seems completely incompatible with what one is working on and then you can interpose it and you end up with something that you hadn't envisaged. I feel quite humbled thinking about Maclauchlan Milne and that insight that he gave me.'[23]

As a founder member of the Young Glasgow Group, Ian McCulloch (b.1935), RSA, was involved in creating a platform for young artists to exhibit their work in Glasgow. Journeying cyclically from representation to abstraction, his later work sets figurative forms within a world of bold colour and pattern.

FIG. 4.4

John Maclauchlan Milne, Harvest Field, Arran

oil on panel, 51 x 60.8 cm / Aberdeen Art Gallery & Museums Collections, Aberdeen
(purchased in 1992 with income from the Webster Bequest and the Jaffrey Fund
© the estate of John Maclauchlan Milne (represented by the Portland Gallery), all rights reserved
image courtesy of Aberdeen Art Gallery & Museums, 2017

FIG. 4.5

Ian McCulloch, Arbroath Harbour, *1957*

ceramic, 35cm diameter / private collection, Scotland / © Ian McCulloch, all rights reserved / image courtesy of the artist

FIG. 4.6

William John Connon,
Farm Cottage near Arbirlot, *1957*

oil on canvas, 40.5 x 61.3 cm / Hospitalfield Collection, Arbroath
© William John Connon, all rights reserved
image courtesy of Hospitalfield, 2017

WILLIAM CONNON RECALLS JAMES MCINTOSH PATRICK AS ARTIST IN RESIDENCE

William Connon (b.1929) was selected to attend the Patrick Allan-Fraser Trust Scheme at Hospitalfield as a student from Gray's School of Art, Aberdeen, in 1957. A significant aspect of this experience was the chance to seek inspiration for his work in the Arbroath and Angus countryside, a practice encouraged by artist in residence James McIntosh Patrick:

'Mr Patrick was an inspiring teacher by example as much as anything and he always kept the dialogue going. We noted how he set about painting in the open air, quickly establishing his colour values as he structured the composition and when the light changed he would continue at length in the studio. Some visual memory!'[24]

Connon's approach to creating a composition from the landscape he observed was also informed by the work and teaching of his tutor at Gray's, Robert Henderson Blyth, whose own experience at Hospitalfield under the tutelage of James Cowie had a formative impact on his development as an artist. The way Connon distilled the forms of the landscape in his painting Farm Cottage near Arbirlot *(fig. 4.6) exemplifies how composition was, for him, as for Blyth and Cowie, an aspect of painting to be emphasised.*

Throughout his career, Connon has continued to be fascinated by techniques of painting, techniques that he passed on to many at Gray's School of Art, where he taught drawing and painting to first–fourth-year students, as well as anatomy and colour theory from 1962 to 1993.

FIG. 4.7

James McIntosh Patrick painting in Arbroath, 1957

private collection, Scotland

and connection to the landscape that resulted from working *en plein air* in North Africa, his painting changed irrevocably.[25] This method of working remained of supreme significance for the rest of his career and, at Hospitalfield, many students followed his example.

One student who seized the opportunity to paint *en plein air* at Hospitalfield was James McIntosh Patrick's daughter, Ann Patrick, who attended in 1957 from Dundee College of Art. Her 1957 *Autumn Landscape* (fig. 4.9) was painted in the fields close to Hospitalfield and captured what she later described as a landscape that was: 'transient ... it only looked like that for a fairly short time.'[26] This practice, and the way in which Patrick captured the subtle shifting of light and shadow through rich earthy tones, connects to the work of the late nineteenth-century Glasgow Boys. *Cabbage Patch* (fig. 4.10), by Patrick's fellow student and future husband Richard Hunter (1935–2014), also evokes the paintings of the Glasgow Boys. His painterly depiction of the cabbage field recalls Guthrie's *A Hind's Daughter* (fig. 3.20) and Melville's *A Cabbage Garden* (fig. 4.8). Patrick posed for the figure in Hunter's painting and, although positioned further into the mid-ground, stands, by accident or design, with the same posture as Melville's figure in *A Cabbage Garden*. Guthrie's sparsely filled field and enigmatic figure present a bleak, raw image; Melville and Hunter use full healthy plants to convey a sense of luscious growth.

While Melville's cabbages are bathed in a warm glow, Hunter's field seems to shine in the strong sunlight. Indeed, Hunter's colour palette is more akin to that of Monet than Melville or the Glasgow Boys. While Hunter began this type of work prior to seeing the exhibition of Monet's work in Edinburgh in the summer of 1957, it is likely that encountering Monet's work added to his point of reference when he painted the Arbroath landscape.[27] Like Monet, Hunter continuously revisited the same subject in order to capture the different effects of changing light. During his *Artist Lives* interview, Hunter described how applying the Impressionists' techniques was a liberating experience that

FIG. 4.8

Arthur Melville, A Cabbage Garden, *1877*

oil on canvas, 45.5 x 30.5 cm / National Galleries of Scotland, Edinburgh (purchased by private treaty sale with the assistance of the Art Fund, 2007) image courtesy of National Galleries of Scotland, 2017

ANN PATRICK RECALLS JAMES MCINTOSH PATRICK AS ARTIST IN RESIDENCE

'While he was at Hospitalfield, he always was going out and painting, which was his norm. We were all going out, cycling into the landscape, painting outside, then coming back in and talking about what we'd been doing and my father taking an interest.

'My father thought it was ridiculous the way people said that his paintings were photographic because he said 'if only I could!' Painting the landscape, you have to choose, sometimes not even consciously knowing why, you have to pick out what it is that is giving you a feeling or an impression of what's there.'[30]

Since her time at Hospitalfield, Ann Patrick (b.1937) has often returned to working en plein air, particularly when travelling across Scotland to paint in Sutherland, Harris and Lewis as well as in Italy. These paintings exemplify her ability to capture changing light and intense colour.

allowed him to emphasise the colour of the landscape and capture the feeling of being within a sea of foliage.[28]

Although Hunter integrated elements from earlier artistic traditions, works like his *Cabbage Patch* should not be considered belated pastiches of nineteenth-century movements. He used a particular aesthetic because it matched his personal response to Hospitalfield's visual environment, a landscape with which he, as a native of Arbroath, had a deep connection. To this effect, McIntosh Patrick observed: 'Richard Hunter has an intimate knowledge of the countryside, its birds, beasts, and human activities which gives a sense of authenticity to his landscapes.'[29] His work should therefore be interpreted as a renewal of tradition within a new context.

The same concept can be applied to the work of McIntosh Patrick. His highly detailed realism should not be dismissed as simply a continuation of conservative representationalism. The detail with which he interpreted the landscape throughout his long career, despite drastic changes in the climate of Scottish painting, reflected his intimate knowledge of every plant and trail of light that fell upon the Angus countryside. This devotion to depicting the 'Angus and Perthshire countryside within a fifteen-mile radius of his home in Dundee'[31] corresponded with his belief that an artist could not be 'a landscape painter in the true sense of the word unless the landscape is very meaningful to you'.[32] This approach corresponded with Fleming's practice, as discussed in the previous chapter. It was also essential to the work of Joan Eardley and James Morrison (b.1932), RSA, RSW, both of whom were also artists in residence

FIG. 4.10
Richard Hunter, Cabbage Patch, *1957*

oil on canvas, 92 x 97 cm / Hospitalfield Collection, Arbroath / / image courtesy of Hospitalfield, 2017

at Hospitalfield, Morrison in 1963 and 1964 and Eardley in 1960. Eardley's statement that 'I find that the more I know a place or the more I know a particular spot, the more I find to paint'[33] and Morrison's assertion that 'I've always felt that you should paint where you are'[34] affirm their commitment to painting the landscapes and communities in which they lived.

Also common to Eardley and Morrison was the place in which they, independently, decided to live and work, the coastal village of Catterline. Throughout the 1950s and 1960s, with Ian Fleming based in Arbroath and then Aberdeen, Eardley and Morrison in Catterline and McIntosh Patrick in Dundee, an emphasis of practice evolved on the northeast coast of Scotland. As McIntosh Patrick, Eardley and Morrison served as artists in residence and Ian Fleming remained connected to the Scheme through its governance after resigning as Warden, Hospitalfield served as a point of connection between them. By enabling these artists to communicate their ideas to groups of students from across Scotland, the Scheme provided an opportunity for aspects of their practice to spread geographically and generationally.

Eardley's early Catterline paintings can be characterised by the colour patches used to abstract the landscape. This aesthetic was reminiscent of the work of the Russian-born, Paris-based twentieth-century painter Nicolas de Staël. His paintings were exhibited in London in 1952 and, four years later, featured at the Society of Scottish Artists' annual exhibition in Edinburgh. His methods of suggesting landscapes and figures without overtly describing them made a significant impact upon mid-century Scottish painters.[35] As Eardley continued to integrate into Catterline and respond to the conditions of painting *en plein air*, often in turbulent weather, her style became increasingly fluid and expressionistic.

It was this style of painting that proved a profound inspiration for 1960 Hospitalfield student Lil Neilson, who was selected to attend from Dundee College of Art. In her report to the Trustees, Eardley described Neilson as a painter who had 'plenty of ability and works hard'.[36] John Cunningham, the other artist in residence that year, concluded in his report that Neilson's paintings captured a 'sense of urgency and activity of the harvest fields against a menacing sky'.[37] This statement provides evidence that Eardley's expressionistic, environmentally reactive painting had an immediate effect upon Neilson's work. After Hospitalfield, Neilson remained in contact with Eardley, joining her in Catterline in 1962. Their paintings from this period[38] bear close resemblance in style and subject. For example, Eardley's *Salmon Net Posts* (fig. 4.11) and Neilson's *Salmon Nets Drying* (fig. 4.12) surround the thick black lines of the posts and nets with vigorous strokes of white, blue and green to suggest the movement and atmosphere of the wind and weather. The differences between their work are subtle. Of the two paintings, Eardley's pushes more strongly towards abstraction, drawing the viewer's attention to the surface and materiality of the painting. For Neilson, Eardley proved a formative artistic influence who was taken far too soon by her untimely death from cancer in 1963.[39]

Although referencing the same source material as Eardley and Neilson, Morrison's distillation of the visual environment of Catterline was distinctive. Prior to settling in and painting Catterline, Morrison lived and worked in Glasgow, interpreting the blackened architecture of the tenements. Works such as his 1959 *Fishing Nets No. 1* (fig. 4.13) relate to his Glasgow painting in their emphasis on line and structure.[40] These characteristics distinguish his paintings from works like Eardley's *Salmon Net Posts*, which allows the paint to exist within a sense of unrestricted space. As with Eardley, Morrison's continual response to and connection with his environment caused the aesthetic of his work to evolve. The sense of containment and structure in his

Glasgow and early Catterline work soon gave way to wide expanses of fields and sky. Using washes of delicate and subtly tonal paint, Morrison abstracted the coastal landscape.[41]

It was at this phase of producing a combination of representational and abstract landscapes that Morrison served as an artist in residence. His 1963 report to the Trustees reveals the ways in which he tried to aid students in what, for many, was their first time dealing with the subject of landscape or working *en plein air*:

> In supervising the course, I divided it into two parts, the first, a period of working quickly on a small scale outside, from the motif, to enable those who had not worked outside before (the majority) to become used to the stronger light and to learn how to establish a convincing key in their painting, the second to use the works and the knowledge gained outside to do more intricate painting whether outside or in the studio.[42]

More than just introducing them to the methods of landscape painting, Morrison shared his own practice with the students: 'When I was at Hospitalfield I painted parts of the grounds ... that seemed to be the way to attract the attention of the students, to actually stand there and paint ... go through the

FIG. 4.12

Lilian Strang Neilson, Salmon Nets Drying

whole processes of, for me, what painting was.'[43]

Morrison's impact upon the students is evident in the work of John Gardiner Crawford (b.1941), RSW, RBA, RI, who attended Hospitalfield in 1963 from Gray's School of Art. The subject of Crawford's 1963 *Drying Nets at Boddin* (fig. 4.14) recalled Morrison's 1959 *Fishing Nets No. 1*, while Crawford's use of line and patches of colour to suggest, rather than directly represent, a landscape related to Morrison's increasing interest in abstraction as well as the work of de Staël. As his career progressed, Crawford's aesthetic favoured detailed realism over abstraction. Taking inspiration from the landscape, particularly that of Arbroath, where he settled in 1972, would remain essential to his artistic process.

Exploring abstraction

Painting in the landscape at Hospitalfield proved a seminal experience for many of the students, yet equally important was the opportunity to experiment with abstraction. In twenty-first-century postmodern Scotland, art can no longer be confined to specific media, scales or aesthetics. From this perspective, it is difficult to comprehend that not that long ago abstract painting was still considered revolutionary. Throughout much of the twentieth century, the Scottish art colleges provided the main source of employment

FIG. 4.13

James Morrison, Fishing Nets No.1, *1959*

oil on panel, 33 x 74 cm / University of Edinburgh Art Collection, Edinburgh: EU0180 (bequeathed by Hope Scott, 1989)

FIG. 4.14

John Gardiner Crawford, Drying Nets at Boddin, *1963*

DAWSON MURRAY REFLECTS ON 1964 AT HOSPITALFIELD

'That first evening I decided to go out and paint. So I took hardboard and my palette and my little portable easel and I just walked out into the field. There were no houses on either side of Hospitalfield, you just walked out into the fields and I walked on for a wee bit and there were some nice little haystacks. I set up my easel and did a very nice little painting, long horizontal one with a little haystack set off to one side and I thought 'Goodness me. This is how Monet must have felt like, discovering his haystacks.'

'It wasn't that long before we had a visit from James Morrison. When he came he'd go out and paint and he was painting in quite an abstract way at that time. He would take his canvases out (and he was using PVA or acrylic) and he'd put a wash of acrylic all over the canvas and then paint into it in broad brush-strokes, painting out in the grounds, an avenue of trees or something, but they were really quite gestural.

'He would come round and have a chat with each of us. I remember he sat down beside me and said, 'You know Dawson, I think you're going to be an abstract painter' and I said, 'I don't think so' (because at that time my favourite painters were Degas, Monet and Sickert). But he saw there were abstract qualities in my paintings, even though they weren't abstract. By the time I left Hospitalfield, I was starting to deal in abstraction and by the time I got back to art school I continued working in abstraction based on observation.

'He wasn't the only artist that we met; there was Dennis Buchan and James Howie as well. Both worked in abstraction or semi-abstraction at the time. He [James Howie] would come 'round the studios and we learned a lot from him. He would say things like 'If you take a little bit of alizarin crimson and some black and mix them and then glaze that area with it and rub it down with a rag, you'll maybe get to what you're after.' Nobody had ever told me to do things like that, but he gave insight into the way the great artists had painted.'[44]

Dawson Murray (b.1944), RSW, RGI, ARE, did indeed develop his enthusiasm for abstraction as a painter and printmaker. The luscious colours and fluidity of works such as Cabbages under Snow draw from the vibrancy and organic forms of nature.

for practising artists in Scotland and juried exhibiting bodies were the only conduits for these artists to display their work and attract public sales.[45] This created a dynamic in which artists trained, taught and exhibited within a relatively self-contained and self-referential system. As the next chapter will discuss, this culture allowed techniques and skills involved in representational painting to be preserved and reinvented. It also meant that innovations in abstraction, such as Picasso and Braque's Cubism or Ben Nicholson's non-representational compositions, were slower to integrate into accepted main-stream visual language. By introducing students to artists in residence who worked in abstraction as well as allowing them to pursue their own aesthetic explorations, the Scheme was a catalyst in the dissemination of abstraction within the culture of Scottish painting.

Debates concerning the merits of abstraction were particularly pervasive among the Hospitalfield students of 1956. That summer the work of Georges Braque, recently made an honorary member of the Royal Scottish Academy, was exhibited at the Edinburgh Festival. When his work was criticised in 'The Letters to the Editor' of *The Glasgow Herald*, the students were motivated to extend such discussions beyond Hospitalfield. Given the artistic conservatism pervasive in Scotland at that time, it is unsurprising that a member of the public wrote to *The Glasgow Herald* of Braque's work: 'If we are told that

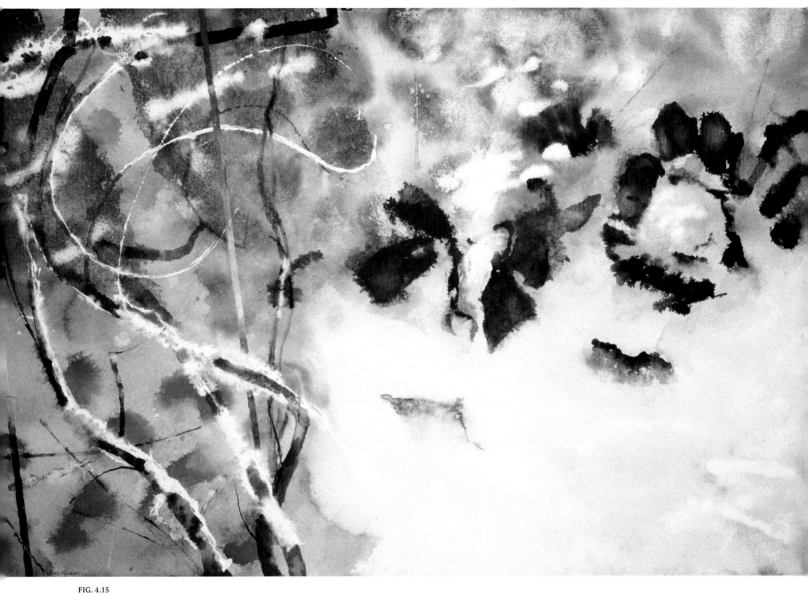

FIG. 4.15

Dawson Murray, Cabbages Under Snow, *2002*

watercolour, 67 x 100 cm / private collection, Scotland / © Dawson Murray, all rights reserved / image courtesy of the artist, 2017

HOSPITALFIELD AND
THE GLASGOW GROUP

The desire among the 1956 Hospitalfield students to broaden the aesthetic range of art in Scotland can be interpreted as having a legacy in connection with The Young Glasgow Group, which many of the 1956 students were instrumental in founding. The Young Glasgow Group's aims of supporting members' artistic experimentation and creating a platform for young painters to display their work was first manifest in their 1958 debut exhibition at Glasgow's McLellan Gallery. The work of Ewen McAslan, Ian McCulloch, Anda Paterson and James Spence, along with that of other recent Glasgow School of Art graduates including Douglas Abercrombie, William Birnie, Margery Clinton, Alan Fletcher, Carole Gibbons, Alasdair Gray, Jack Knox, James Morrison and James Watt, was displayed in an egalitarian fashion, rather than relying on a juried committee. Exhibitors drew lots for space on the gallery walls, which each artist then curated as they wished with work of their choosing, be it abstract or figurative.

Their initiative to create exhibiting opportunities, increase the presence of art within their native city, and support each other in pursuit of their individual aesthetics, should be considered a precedent for the type of grassroots movements that have contributed to the development of art in Glasgow from the twentieth into the twenty-first century.[50]

an incomprehensible jumble of squares, triangles, fish and chips represents the struggles of the artist's soul against frustrations, we are not impressed.'[46] In response, the students defended Braque as 'the great colourist of Europe, the greatest visual poet of our time', and invited the public to engage in dialogue about modern art, 'for we believe that art was never more needing in our society than today'.[47] Their letter succeeded in provoking a dialogue. For several weeks, 'Letters to the Editor' appeared in *The Glasgow Herald*, each presenting different views on Braque's work and the place of abstraction within the tradition of Scottish painting.[48] The impact of such discussions went beyond a period of youthful rebellion, with Ian McCulloch recalling that the time at Hospitalfield 'was a turning point for a lot of us'.[49]

It would be an oversimplification, however, to conclude that Scotland's art colleges and exhibition bodies and those of the United Kingdom were completely averse to abstraction. This is exemplified by the work of 1955 Hospitalfield student Moira Maitland (1936–2004). At Hospitalfield, Maitland encountered the artist in residence James Bateman and their work could not have been more different. Bateman's style was one of realistic clarity through which he depicted the English landscape and scenes of daily life, while Maitland's only hinted at the visual world through colour and geometry. While Maitland's paintings were probably those that Bateman later referred to in his report to the Trustees as having 'absurd shape', the majority of his assessment contained praise rather than criticism: 'Moira Maitland is a most sensitive and gifted student. She has imagination and a delicacy of feeling.'[51] It therefore seems that, although artistic difference could have led to conflict, Bateman's supportive, rather than dogmatic, approach allowed Maitland and her classmates to develop their own aesthetics freely. Maitland's continuation of experimentations in abstraction on returning to Gray's School of Art to complete her Post-Diploma further suggests that there was a place for abstraction in Scottish art education, although perhaps only for the advanced student at this time.

While in the minority, select members of the faculties of the Scottish art colleges were devoted to working in languages of abstraction. One such faculty member, from Edinburgh College of Art, was James Cumming, RSA, RSW (1922–1991), who served as artist in residence in 1961 and 1962. Cumming's language of abstraction emerged from early twentieth-century British and European modernism, evolving alongside Scottish contemporaries Alan Davie, Wilhemina Barns-Graham and fellow faculty member and former Hospitalfield student Charles Pulsford. During Cumming's residencies, he introduced students to contemporary developments in abstraction as well as his personal methodologies. His 1962 report to the Trustees detailed how 'Lectures accompanied by colour transparencies filled thirteen hours of the first ten-day visit in July. The theme was chosen to help advanced appreciation of contemporary painting ... Technical instruction was given later',[52] and went on to specify the type of technical instruction and the precise time spent on each activity. The rigour this structure suggests was even more evident in his individual tutorials with students that he believed 'provided the best technique of individual development'.[53]

The 1961 Hospitalfield student Alexander Fraser, RSA, RSW, recalled the challenging nature of the exercises Cumming set them, but concluded that he 'underwent a metamorphosis, probably because of the questions Cumming was posing'.[54] One manifestation of this process of metamorphosis was Fraser's 1963 *Untitled* painting (fig. 4.16), featuring a Celtic cross. This painting, like Cumming's 1962 *The Longshoreman's Dream* (fig. 4.17), used

FIG. 4.16

Alexander Fraser, Untitled, c.*1963*

oil on board, 91 x 129.2 cm / Art & Heritage Collection of Robert Gordon University, Aberdeen (acquired from the artist when a student)
© Alexander Fraser, all rights reserved / image courtesy of Robert Gordon University, 2017

FIG. 4.17

James Cumming, The Longshoreman's Dream, *1962*

oil on canvas, 101.5 x 152.5 cm / Aberdeen Art Gallery & Museums Collections, Aberdeen (purchased in 1962 with the aid of a grant from the Calouste Gulbenkian Foundation)
© the artist's estate, all rights reserved / image courtesy of Aberdeen Art Gallery & Museums, 2017

the visual world as the starting point for what developed into an abstracted composition of colour, form and line. As with *The Longshoreman's Dream*, Fraser's painting suggests something more fundamental about the character of the subject beyond its visual qualities through abstraction. The lasting impact of Fraser's experience at Hospitalfield can be seen as he continued to develop various languages of abstraction throughout his career. Works like his 1974 *Stonehaven* used geometry to distil an observed environment into essential forms. In contrast, paintings such as his 1983 *Guild Street No. 3* employed a gestural exploration of pure colour. Different still was the way in which colour, form and beautifully rendered figuration interact in compositions like his 2002 *Family Gathering*. Regardless of its specific incarnation, Fraser's understanding of abstraction has enabled him to create painted dimensions of dynamic form and ambiguous meaning, and has continued to inform his practice.

Cumming's example also had a profound impact on Fraser's fellow Hospitalfield student, John Byrne. As Robert Hewison detailed in *John Byrne: Art and Life*, Byrne was so inspired by Cumming's approach to abstraction, which seemed to him far more progressive than the teaching at Glasgow School of Art, that he left Glasgow and enrolled at Edinburgh College of Art the following year. Byrne soon found, however, that the curriculum at Edinburgh, despite Cumming's presence, was just as strict and structured as it had been in Glasgow.[55] Although this experience may seem to indicate that Hospitalfield negatively impacted Byrne, who subsequently returned to Glasgow School of Art to finish his diploma, it emphasises how Hospitalfield's progressive creative environment allowed both students and teachers to experiment beyond the conservative structure of the art colleges' curricula. Furthermore, it exemplifies how this generation of young artists was eager to engage with developments in contemporary painting.

While Braque's Cubism caused debate among the Scottish public and arts community and Cumming's experimentations with abstraction represented a minority within a more pervasively representational culture of painting, the reception of American Abstract Expressionism was even more controversial. As the Second World War and British post-war austerity prevented free international artistic exchange, Abstract Expressionism did not enter the artistic sphere of Scottish artists until the late 1950s. Abstract Expressionism was a radical movement, not only because it aesthetically challenged what art could be, but because its American origin also challenged British national identity, so essential to much of British wartime and post-war art.[56] British painters' experimentations with these new aesthetics and techniques caused a crisis of identity. When reflecting on this transitional period in *British Painting 1952–1977*, Royal Academician Frederic Gore concluded: 'the immediate difficulty for the public and critics was that the paintings seemed either too American or not enough.'[57]

British artists' interest in this new style and method of working would, however, eventually outweigh initial cultural reservations. Throughout the 1960s and 1970s, many of Hospitalfield's 1950s and 1960s participants, such as Jack Knox, Ian McKenzie Smith, Ian McCulloch, Alexander Fraser, Dennis Buchan and William Littlejohn,[58] assimilated aspects of Abstract Expressionism within their own practices. Through their work and their teaching, Abstract Expressionism, and abstraction more generally, became a more pervasive visual idiom and was introduced to art students at an earlier stage in their education. Some insight into the impact of Abstract Expressionism on Hospitalfield was contained in John Miller's 1967 report to the Trustees, which highlighted how the scale of the students' work had increased since his time as a student at Hospitalfield under James Cowie: 'the studio accommodation

ALAN ROBB REFLECTS ON 1968 AT HOSPITALFIELD

'The unexpected bonus for me coming to Hospitalfield in the summer of '68 was Jack Knox, our summer tutor. It was during that time that I began to consider a more abstract approach to my painting. I continued to work on location, but with a more selective approach emphasising the structures of things, reducing the number of elements present and departing from local colour. The Hospitalfield Scholarship came at the right time for me. Jack was there almost every day painting in the barn down at the bottom of the paddock. So I would go down there, keen and curious, and we became quite friendly. He was painting in acrylic and showed me how he was mixing his own primer and working with raw pigments and copolymer emulsion as a binder. All very different from oils, much more systematic. He asked my opinion of what he was doing. It was really great. I think the success of a lot of the adventurous painting that was going on in Dundee was due to him.

'But I think the glory days were where you took your materials and you walked down to the harbour and you set up and you worked all day, learning how light changes over a period working outside, that something you're looking at in the morning is so different in the afternoon ... that you've got to develop a way of painting that can follow that and make those changes. I think that's such an interesting thing to learn.'[59]

The evolution of the work of Alan Robb (b.1946), RSA, RSW, *through various incarnations of aesthetic exemplifies his continual reconsideration and integration of the styles, techniques, and imagery of the art of the past and art on the forefront of contemporary practice.*

is now greater than formerly, but the large size of the canvases could make the studios quite cramped if all the students were working indoors at one time.'[60]

The Scottish art world was changing and so too was Hospitalfield. Reid would not, however, be the one to oversee this. In 1970, he retired after sixteen years as Warden. During this period, Hospitalfield had been a place where students could discover new ways of working, learn from one another and gain new insights through the artists in residence. From this firmament came innovations in landscape and abstract painting. With new students and artists in residence arriving each year, the Hospitalfield experience was becoming a unifying point among many in Scotland's artistic community.

When George Washington Browne argued for the closure of the Allan-Fraser Art College and the dissolution of Hospitalfield as a site for artists' residency in the late 1920s, he believed that such a small-scale community and remote location was detrimental to young artists and could not impact Scottish art. While the specificity of Hospitalfield's art programme had changed fifty years on, its influence on individuals and Scottish art more broadly was demonstrating that Browne had been incorrect in his conclusion. As noted by John Miller, who attended Hospitalfield as a student from Glasgow School of Art under James Cowie and returned for a brief residency in 1967: 'Mr. Reid has compiled a list of the students who have attended the College since its rebirth ... a glance at this list which contains many of the established and up and coming artists of Scotland does, I feel, justify Patrick Allan-Fraser's Bequest.'[61] As the years continued to pass and the number of former Hospitalfield students with critically and commercially successful artistic careers grew, Miller's assertion that Hospitalfield was an incubator for young talent would become increasingly evident.

5

Expanding connections and new challenges
The Patrick Allan-Fraser Trust Scheme 1970–94

Assisting students on their journeys of artistic and self-discovery had always been central to the Scheme's mission. For over three decades, it allowed young artists to develop their personal practice, learn within a community of peers, and seek inspiration within a stimulating visual environment. The particular realisation of these outcomes was influenced by each Warden's approach. Cowie and Fleming had led by example, encouraging students to pursue practices that aligned with their own affinities. Reid and the artists in residence then implemented a less focused, but more varied, programme. During this period, Hospitalfield's connection to the local community and emphasis on landscape painting continued, while also increasingly encouraging experimentation with abstraction. In many ways these developments continued to evolve under the following successive Wardens: Malcolm Fryer, holding the position from 1970 to 1976, and William Payne, from 1976 to 1994. As Fryer and Payne focused their attentions on the managerial aspect of the Warden's role, the arrangement of inviting annual artists in residence continued. This offered students the opportunity for independent work, exchange and an introduction to the new ideas brought by the artists in residence. While many of these continued to be artists from Scotland, an increasing number of international participants now appeared. This greater diversity introduced students to a wider variety of approaches. In addition, it connected Hospitalfield to an ever-widening sphere of artists within an increasingly international art world.

In tandem with these developments, the future financial and educational viability of the Scheme was proving ever more uncertain. In 1969, the Scottish Education Department (SED) became concerned that the Secretary of State's review of Educational Endowments could conclude that the Scheme was doing too little for too few. In response, the SED issued a series of ambitious recommendations. These fell into three categories: increasing 'the contact between young artists and Hospitalfield'; renovating Hospitalfield House; and securing viable income streams for the future.[1] The Trustees supported the fulfilment of the recommendations, but, as they remained connected with Hospitalfield in mainly an advisory capacity, the task of orchestrating how such goals could be met, and then meeting them, became a new facet of the Warden's responsibilities. As a system of accountability to measure the achievement of organisational aims or growth had never been established between the SED, the Trustees and the Warden, the implementation of changes was continually fraught with uncertainty and conflict. Subsequently, an undercurrent of doubt was pervasive throughout Fryer's and Payne's periods as Warden. Each attempted to define Hospitalfield's educational relevance and secure its financial viability, but neither reached a successful resolution. Despite the continual institutional challenges during these years, the Scheme remained an integral part of Scottish art education and continued to be beneficial to many students' development.

Carel Victor Morlais Weight, The Return – Conversation, *1950–74*

oil on hardboard, 60.9 x 76 cm / Aberdeen Art Gallery & Museum Collection, Aberdeen (purchased 1975)

Malcolm Fryer: Warden 1970–76

Trained at Lancaster School of Art, Malcolm Fryer (b.1937) was a painter who actively exhibited in the north of England, guest lectured at Blackpool Art College and, from 1967, served as curator of the Haworth Art Gallery in Accrington. With the Warden's remit becoming increasingly diversified, it was likely that the Trustees were encouraged by his broad skill set to select him for the role. As Fryer was primarily a landscape painter, Hospitalfield's setting was conducive to his continued practice. While he painted throughout his time as Warden, Fryer did not exhibit in Scotland or offer students guidance in the way Cowie or Fleming had. It is probable that this was both a personal choice[2] and a result of the shifting emphasis of the Warden's responsibilities from an artistic guide to a site manager.

Once the SED had issued its recommendations, expanding Hospital-field's programming beyond the Scheme became a new critical facet of the Warden's job. Fryer saw the potential to increase activities and income not only by working with visual artists but also by attracting writers and musicians. Considering his family connections, this is perhaps unsurprising. His brother, Fritz Fryer, was the guitarist with The Four Pennies, whose 1964 number one hit 'Juliette' was named after Malcolm's daughter. Following along these lines, Fryer initiated a series of programmes including chamber music concerts, joint programmes with the Arbroath Art Society, short courses for art college students and Local Educational Authority art courses. At the centre of Hospitalfield's newly expanded calendar remained the long-standing arrangement outlined by the Scheme. In Fryer's discussions with staff from the four Scottish art colleges,

> It was agreed that the present summer course was of great value, and should not be changed ... There was a strong, almost fervent, feeling that Hospitalfield should always be a fine art establishment and that the unique atmosphere of the place should be preserved at all costs.[3]

Throughout this period of transition when new programmes were being introduced and the traditions of the Scheme continued, three trends emerged: a renewed connection with English Art, the cultivation of a sense of localism, and the encouragement of students' artistic independence.

In the last year of Reid's Wardenship, 1970, the English painter Cyril Reason was invited to be artist in residence. This began a revival of the relationship between Hospitalfield and English artists, something Fryer's appointment compounded. Reason was trained at the Royal College of Art (RCA) from 1951 to 1954 and, at the time of his residency, held a fellowship at Nottingham College of Art. Whether his or a Trustees' connection to the RCA helped to cultivate a new connection between Hospitalfield and the RCA is unknown, but the subsequent residencies of Peter Blake, CBE, RDI, RA, and Carel Weight (1908–97), CH, CBE, RA, suggest that an institutional bond was formed.

Peter Blake is perhaps most recognised for his images that responded to popular culture: targets, wrestlers, pin-up girls and celebrities. Blake's three summers at Hospitalfield, however, aligned with a period of his practice when the countryside and country living, rather than the urban environment, provided inspiration for his work. This change in imagery was intrinsically connected to a change in lifestyle, as he sought to distance himself from London and relocated to Wellow, near Bath. There he became instrumental in the formation of the Brotherhood of Ruralists, a collective of artists including Blake, David Inshaw, Ann Arnold, Graham Arnold, Annie Ovenden and Graham Ovenden, who exhibited together and went on annual art excursions.

ARTISTS IN RESIDENCE

1971: Robert Callender
1972: Richard Hunter and William Littlejohn
1973: Peter Blake
1974: Carel Weight
1975: Peter Blake
1976: Peter Blake

FIG. 5.2

Eugeniusz Jarych, Elliot Beach, Arbroath, *1974*

oil and sand on canvas, 39.4 x 48.2 cm / private collection, Scotland
© Eugeniusz Jarych, all rights reserved / image courtesy of the artist, 2017

EUGENIUSZ JARYCH ON PAINTING THE LANDSCAPE

Eugeniusz Jarych was selected to attend the Patrick Allan-Fraser Trust Scheme from Dundee College of Art in 1974. During his time at Hospitalfield, he often sought out the surrounding landscape as inspiration for his work and recalls Carel Weight, artist in residence that summer, as a memorable and sage presence:

'On arrival at Hospitalfield, I recollect being amazed to see such a grand building with turrets, sculpted heads, black iron dogs in various places and high up on the building facing the walled garden, a sun dial decorated on three sides. Immediately, the latter seemed to set the scene for me as I felt at that moment, it was 'our' time. We had three months in which to explore and hone our creativity surrounded by beautiful carvings, trees, a fernery and a walled garden, bounded by woodlands and fields much more expansive then than they are today. This gave me a sense of being somewhere quite isolated and very special which felt positive and life-affirming.

'What I very much wanted to do was paint landscapes and they were not part of the course at Duncan of Jordanstone. I could see the sea from my bedroom window at Hospitalfield and one day I ventured out with my canvas. This painting was a bit of an experiment of putting the natural elements of the place, which in-cluded sand, into the oil paint and then onto the canvas. Another painting reflected my fascination for the pebbles on the beach. The pattern of the myriad of pebbles of various sizes and colours gave a softness to the high bank of the beach with a hint of blue sky and wisps of white clouds, contrasting with the russet of the withered Dock weeds. My largest seascape, which was four feet by three feet, lay unfinished. Thirty-five years later it was completed to become the catalyst for a travelling exhibition of fifty seascapes painted at Elliot Beach, Arbroath.'[4]

The natural world continues to play an important role in the work of Eugeniusz Jarych, who has often drawn inspiration from memories and recollections of landscapes.

Although their purpose was never formally defined, they were joined by a shared commitment to rural life, an interest in artistically responding to the pastoral landscape in which they lived, and connecting with the history of English painting. This final affinity was reflected in their name, which evolved from a conversation about which of the Pre-Raphaelite Brotherhood each would have been. It also alluded to other previous 'Brotherhoods' of British art such as the Brotherhood of Ancients. Blake's imagery of this period recalled and reinvented the type of fairies, myths and stories that captured the imagination of his nineteenth-century predecessors.[5] It is therefore unsurprising that Hospitalfield, with its pastoral setting and Victoriana, was an attractive locale for Blake at this point in his career.

While Blake's time at Hospitalfield corresponded with his investigation of ruralism, Carel Weight's residency aligned with a productive period of painting following his retirement from the RCA. During this phase, he continued to explore motifs of tragedy, comedy, angst, surprise and turmoil through the human dramas that played out on his canvases.[6] Although full of imagination, his work was always rooted in reality and Hospitalfield's varied landscape would have provided him with ample stimulus. For instance, the Hospitalfield studios form the backdrop for his 1950–74 painting *The Return – Conversation* (fig. 5.1), in which the viewer is drawn into the mystery of the exchange between the two women and from where and what circumstances they are returning.

Given the date of the painting, Weight's encounter with Hospitalfield and its surrounds before his residency in 1974 was most likely the result of an introduction to the site during his time as an external examiner for one of the Scottish art schools, an occurrence which was not uncommon given the art schools' connection with Hospitalfield. Although Weight declined the offer of the opportunity to serve as artist in residence in 1956 and it is impossible to speculate the effect his influence would have had upon that group of students, certainly, nearly two decades later, he found Hospitalfield once more an inspiring situation to work in and was able to share his vast knowledge, insight and experience of British art with a later generation of students.

Connections with Blake and Weight reinvigorated Hospitalfield's relationship with English painting. Simultaneously, the Scheme's engagement with the artistic community of Arbroath continued to be cultivated. This bond was not the result of provincialism, but rather a sign of vibrant localism. Through the years, the activity of the Arbroath Art Society, the dedication of the art staff at Arbroath High School, and the population of artists living in Arbroath – including Talbert McLean, John McLean, George Grassie, Robert Cargill, Ann Patrick (Hunter), Richard Hunter, Joan Cuthill, Irene Halliday and William Littlejohn – contributed to this creative environment. Inviting Richard Hunter and William Littlejohn to be artists in residence and encouraging Hospitalfield students to exhibit at the annual Arbroath Art Society Exhibition fostered continued rapport. In addition, Cargill and Dundee-based artists like Neil Dallas Brown and Dennis Buchan frequented Hospitalfield, adding to the artistic milieu and exchange there.

Cargill, Hunter and Littlejohn were not only native to Arbroath and connected to its community, but used the shoreline, the harbour and the atmosphere of Arbroath to inspire much of their work. During his time as a student at Hospitalfield in 1956 and 1957, Hunter displayed an affinity for responding to the way the ever-changing quality of light illuminated the forms and colours of the landscape. Turning from the agricultural fields to the harbour, Hunter's more mature work, whether representational or abstract, captured the essence of place with a sensitivity that could only have been acquired by familiarity and constant observation. Pushing further into abstraction

FIG. 5.3
Robert Cargill, Environment Painting, *1974/5*

oil and mixed media on canvas, 106.5 x 86 cm / Hospitalfield Collection, Arbroath / © the artist's estate, all rights reserved / image courtesy of Hospitalfield, 2017

FIG. 5.4

Allan Beveridge, The Gateway, Hospitalfield, *1976*

and blurring the lines between painting and sculpture, Cargill also sought to capture *genius loci*, the spirit of place. By incorporating objects and materials found on the shoreline into his work, as in *Environment Painting* (fig. 5.3), he created physical and conceptual links between the artwork and the place that inspired it. In doing this, he expressed the deep connection he felt for the northeastern coastline, a landscape in which he lived and that had been home to generations of his ancestors.

Littlejohn's work also reflected his relationship with Arbroath and Hospitalfield. First attending Hospitalfield in 1946 during James Cowie's Wardenship, his sketches from this period reveal his interest in Cowie's aesthetic and method.[7] While Littlejohn's work increasingly developed a more abstract aesthetic trajectory, the continued importance of composition in his distillation of observed places and objects into line, colour and form can be seen as a result of Cowie's lasting influence. As an art teacher in Arbroath and, later, as Head of Drawing and Painting at Gray's School of Art, Littlejohn passed on artistic skills and approaches, some of which he learned from Cowie.

Both the legacy of Cowie's influence and the opportunity for interpreting the landscape that Hospitalfield provided is made evident by comparing Cowie's *c.*1940–4 *Evening Star* (fig. 3.1), Littlejohn's 1962 *Evening Star III* (fig. 5.5) and Allan Lawson's 1971 *Dickman's Den* (fig. 5.6).[8] The cool palette of *Evening Star III*, along with its title, recalls Cowie's painting. Furthermore, the way the shapes and lines lead the eye into a central point of focus compares to Cowie's composition. The sense of looking through an opening at a view also features in Lawson's *Dickman's Den*. As a student of Littlejohn's at Gray's School of Art, Lawson would have been familiar with his teacher's work. His particular mode of abstraction in *Dickman's Den* is akin to Littlejohn's in *Evening Star III*. Both paintings use shapes, lines and a restricted, but tonally rich, colour palette to suggest the forms and experience of landscape. Lawson's later abstract work, such as his 1981 *A Slow Melting*, which won the Shell Prize when exhibited at the Aberdeen Artists Society, owe much of their dynamism to composition. This lineage of pictorial emphasis exemplifies how Hospitalfield served as a point of connection and transference through multiple generations of artists.

Engaging with the landscape that inspired these artists, as well as countless other previous Hospitalfield participants, continued to be an integral part of the students' experience. This was the case for Allan Beveridge (1944– 2017), who attended in 1976 from Duncan of Jordanstone College of Art and Design in Dundee. Inspired by the landscape surrounding Hospitalfield, and having recently developed an interest in the work of British and French nineteenth- and early twentieth-century Realist painters, he was attracted to painting *en plein air*. The freedom of brushstrokes and sensitivity to changing light in his painting *The Gateway, Hospitalfield* (fig. 5.4) embody his response to the conditions of painting outdoors. They also related to the aesthetic of the Glasgow Boys, whose work he frequently saw at the Kelvingrove Art Gallery while growing up in Glasgow. In this way, *The Gateway* embodies how the Scheme promoted a continuation and reinvigoration of the Scottish landscape tradition. It also marked the beginning of a practice of seeking source material from the landscape, which would remain an essential aspect of Beveridge's creative process.[9]

As well as offering students the opportunity to encounter new influences and engage with the landscape, Hospitalfield continued to be, as the Trustees described, 'a place where they [the students] might come and in total-ly different, relaxed and fairly comfortable surroundings, test out their self-

FIG. 5.5

William Hunter Littlejohn, Evening Star III, *1962*

oil on canvas, 60 x 90.5 cm / The Stirling Smith Art Gallery and Museum, Stirling (gift from the Friends of the Smith, 1979)
© the artist's estate/Bridgeman Images, all rights reserved / image courtesy of The Stirling Smith Art Gallery and Museum

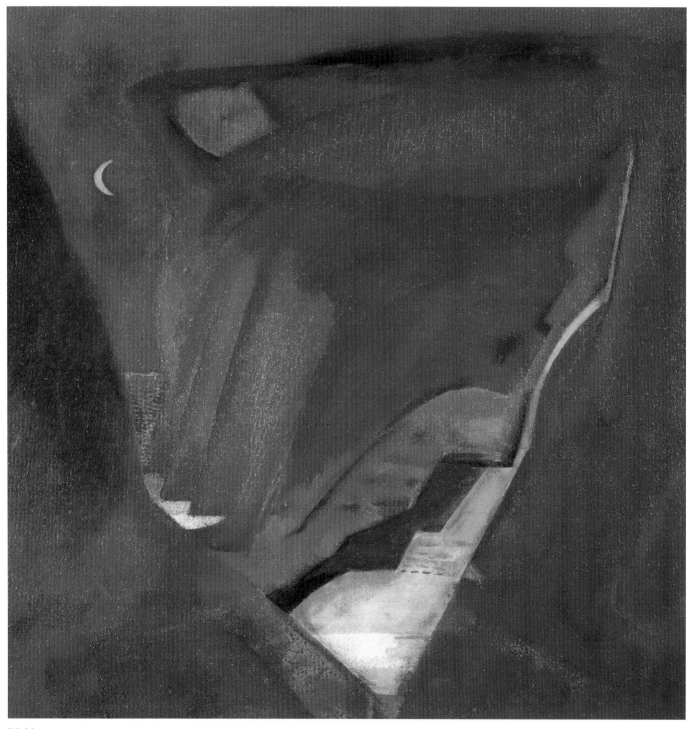

FIG. 5.6

Allan Lawson, Dickman's Den, *1971*

reliance as artists'.[10] This was a particularly important aspect of the Patrick Allan-Fraser Trust Scheme because it provided a contrasting experience to that of the art school environment. Although the art world had changed significantly since the beginning of the century, by the 1970s, the curricula of the Scottish art colleges still retained much of its early twentieth-century structure. Students of drawing and painting continued to be taught a skills-based programme of how to approach the genres of figuration, still-life and composition. By providing a time where students could choose their own foci and methods of working, Hospitalfield was an opportunity for students to explore their own visions.

The positive impact of this opportunity is exemplified by the experiences of Janet Tod (b.1948), who was selected to participate in the Scheme from Duncan of Jordanstone College of Art and Design in 1971. When reflecting upon this period, Tod emphasised the importance of being able 'to have that time, the freedom to not have the set agenda or timetable that one had at the college — just to be able to paint'.[11] With this new-found freedom, Tod gravitated toward the gardens and her *Greenhouse, 1971* (fig. 5.7) exemplifies the type of colour-rich, vibrant paintings that were produced as a result of personal artistic vision and visual stimulus.

After her initial summer in 1971, Tod returned for several successive summers as the cook, and when not attending to her catering duties, she was able to paint in the small attic studio above the main studio where the rest of the students worked. Particularly inspired to return to the gardens, Tod produced a body of work that enabled her to gain a British Council scholarship to travel, work and study in Yugoslavia.

Although Tod's aesthetics and artistic interests have evolved over time, connections to her Hospitalfield work can still be seen in her continued bold use of colour in the depiction of all things that grow. Furthermore, in the midst of preparing for her 2015 exhibition at London's Russell Gallery, Tod identified her time at Hospitalfield as 'hugely significant', concluding, 'I'm still painting and I don't know if that would have happened without the Hospitalfield experience.'[12]

Similarly, Kate Whiteford, OBE (b.1952), who attended from Glasgow School of Art in 1972, concluded that Hospitalfield was a beneficial opportunity because of the visual stimuli and creative environment it provided for students with ambitions to develop their work. In addition, the distinctive quality of light that entered the Hospitalfield studios, which was particularly conducive for painting, left a lasting impression upon Whiteford. When commissioning her own London studio, designed by Richard Nightingale in 1998,[13] she recalled the importance of the ambience of the light-filled Hospitalfield studios.

While the Scheme was still proving beneficial to students, Hospitalfield as an institution continued to struggle in its fulfilment of the SED's 1969 recommendations. A sustainable financial model that could support the costs of preserving the historic elements of Hospitalfield House while making it suitable for hosting a greater number of artists and events had not been successfully formulated. This meant that selling land and assets, the historic method for supplementing low income, was once again relied upon as a short-term solution. With diminishing land-holdings and saleable assets, this option was becoming less lucrative and less viable for the future. The effects of these tensions were at times palpable within the atmosphere at Hospitalfield throughout Fryer's tenure as Warden and contributed to his resignation in 1976.

LENNOX DUNBAR ON HOSPITALFIELD'S STUDIOS

In addition to providing a setting sympathetic to painting, the individual space each student occupied in the studios further cultivated a sense of artistic independence. This is exemplified by the experience of Lennox Dunbar (b.1952), RSA and Emeritus Professor of Fine Art at Gray's School of Art, a student of Gray's School of Art who was selected to participate in the Patrick Allan-Fraser Trust Scheme in 1973:

'I saw it as an opportunity, as most did, to use the studio to the fullest potential that we could. (And my memory was there was a little studio that also had a printing press to use, if you were interested, to make prints, which I did, on occasion.) The studios were much bigger than the space that one had as an undergraduate in Aberdeen. Suddenly you had this big studio and there were only four of you in it and you could leave stuff out. That was the first experience I'd had of something that was territorially mine because the way it was orchestrated at Gray's was that you would come in the morning and you would grab a space and you would start to paint and you then would put your stuff away at night. So you didn't really have a kind of studio as such, it wasn't your area that you could reflect on the next morning when you came in. You had to haul everything out again. So the Hospitalfield studios were ideal, it was terrific.'[14]

For Lennox Dunbar, Hospitalfield provided a step on his artistic journey, throughout which he would attain numerous awards and bursaries to exhibit and develop work in Scotland and internationally.

William Payne: Warden 1976–94

Upon Fryer's departure, William Payne[15] was appointed interim Warden, becoming permanently situated in the position in 1979. Payne first came to Hospitalfield during Fryer's Wardenship as part of an initiative to document and revalue its contents and collections. Trained at the Ruskin School of Drawing before achieving a Bachelor of Arts from the University of East Anglia, Payne, although not a practising artist, brought with him an enthusiasm for both art and history. This initial interest in the historic elements of Hospitalfield House and a belief in their significance impacted his outlook on Hospitalfield's future, particularly as the organisation's mission was more frequently called into question.

Just as discussions among the Trustees of the Allan-Fraser Art College concerning Hospitalfield's fiscal failures soon raised enquiry into its educational value, so too did Payne and the Trustees of the 1970s begin to query the relevance of the Scheme. Other opportunities for students' artistic development, such as Edinburgh College of Art's Grant scholarship, had run concurrently with Hospitalfield for much of the twentieth century, but the increase in the number of opportunities, like Glasgow School of Art's partnership programme with Culzean Castle, meant the Hospitalfield experience was in danger of becoming viewed as less significant unless its offerings and impact were clarified.[16] Despite discussions and investigations by Payne and the Trustees, clarification never occurred and a strategic action plan was never realised. Although in the coming years, Hospitalfield increasingly hosted conferences, partnership projects and short courses, these were not sufficiently lucrative to support the institution's running costs. They also lacked thematic focus, doing little to support or improve the arrangement between Hospitalfield and the four Scottish art colleges, which, according to the newly revised Patrick Allan-Fraser Trust Scheme of 1980, remained its primary mission.[17]

Despite institutional turmoil and growing financial concerns, the opportunities the Scheme provided continued to have a positive impact upon the students. By enabling them to develop their individual practices, work in a new visual environment and engage with a community of artists, the Scheme remained relevant to students' creative growth and the Scottish system of art education. One student to benefit from these opportunities was Gwen Hardie, who attended in 1982 from Edinburgh College of Art. With the time and freedom to produce self-directed work in a visually stimulating setting, Hardie painted a series of self-portraits. Some of these responded to the changing light, which she observed by returning to the same vantage point at different times of the day. Others were inspired by the various perspectives and spaces that could be found within Hospitalfield House. For Hardie, Hospitalfield provided another step toward developing figurative imagery within a personal visual language.

In hindsight, Hardie's interest in the human form can be contextualised within a trend in Scottish painting towards New Figuration that was pervasive throughout the 1980s and 1990s.[18] The Scottish art colleges' continued educational emphasis on skill-based learning in traditional genres of image-making was an essential facet of the cultivation of this generation of painters, whose figurative work achieved national and international acclaim. That the vast majority of students to participate in the Scheme during this period continued to be students of drawing and painting paralleled this trend.

Among this generation of figurative painters to utilise the chance for independent work which Hospitalfield provided was Peter Howson, OBE (b.1958). As Robert Heller described in his book *Peter Howson*: 'Howson's development as an artist moved forward decisively after the summer of 1979 ... Howson feels now, as he did then, that he made a breakthrough at Hospitalfield, which gave him the launching pad for his return to art school.'[19] Like Ken Currie, Adrian Wiszniewski and Steven Campbell, Howson was a student at Glasgow School of Art who was encouraged by art teacher Sandy Moffat to develop his interest in using the human figure to create bold, thought-provoking images. The germination of his particular affinity for depicting the heroism, masculinity and brutality of soldiers was reflected in the many studies and several paintings of the Royal Marines based near Hospitalfield.

Throughout this period, the Scheme fostered students' exploration of their independent creative visions. Continuing to invite artists in residence, however, meant that they were not left entirely unsupported. Under Payne, it became increasingly common for several artists to undertake shorter residencies within one summer. A greater number of influences meant students had the opportunity to be exposed to a wider variety of outlooks, but in a less focused or consistent way. Within this more diverse artistic spectrum, two trends of influence emerged from this period.

GWEN HARDIE RECALLS 1982 AT HOSPITALFIELD

'I started work early in the mornings and recall mornings of glorious sunshine, it was wonderful to be so close to the sea and the beautiful sand dunes — incorporating a daily walk into the schedule of working. I would work on self-portraits in different settings sometimes based on the light. For example, I would do a self-portrait at 8 a.m. one day, the next from exactly the same vantage point at 9 a.m. etc. Other times I would base the self-portrait on unusual vantage points around the grand house; I recall painting myself through a huge mirror in one of the grand rooms and my head is a tiny part of the lower corner of this mirror.

'I think we had communal lunches and dinners, though I recall the dinners more — 12 of us all sharing meals every day — it was very interesting to meet students from the other colleges. It was a self-determined schedule apart from mealtimes, which made a big difference to how one organised one's day. There were no tutors, advice, exams; so obviously a very different experience, one in which you had to be more self-reliant. I think it fostered significant development in the direction of one's own autonomy.

'One couldn't help becoming more actively engaged with one's fundamental reason to work. It felt like all the obstacles and distractions to working had gone, which, in some ways, presented a new sort of challenge, one entirely to do with self-motivation. I think it brought a new intensity of focus to my practice and strengthened my resolve to make art central to my life.'[20]

The commitment to art that Gwen Hardie (b.1962) displayed during her time at Hospitalfield led to her developing an admirable reputation in Scotland and abroad. Her exploration of the human form, which began during her time as a student, invites a new way of thinking about the figure which transforms the objectifying gaze. Her work is represented in many public collections such as the Metropolitan Museum, New York, and The Scottish National Gallery of Modern Art in Edinburgh.

The first trend involved former Hospitalfield students returning as artists in residence. With the Scheme over forty years old, it is unsurprising that numerous previous Hospitalfield students, selected to attend based on their talent and commitment to art, had since developed burgeoning careers and were now credible residency candidates. This experience of return prompted many of these former Hospitalfield students to be particularly perceptive of differences between the artistic interests, patterns of working and group dynamics they had experienced and those of the new generation. Their comparisons provide insight into ways in which the application of the Scheme had evolved and how, in many cases, this reflected changes and continuities in art education, Scottish painting and Scottish culture.

Along with the continued participation of artists in residence from Scotland and England, a new dynamic of exchange between Hospitalfield and the United States was the second distinctive trend of this period. This connection was largely due to the transatlantic transfer of the Hospitalfield Trustee Anthony Jones from his role as Director of Glasgow School of Art (1981–5) to the School of the Art Institute of Chicago (SAIC). It also aligned with Payne's desire to cultivate relationships with American universities to establish lucrative income streams. For many students, the opportunity to engage with the American artists in residence provided new perspectives through which they could approach their work.

This is exemplified by the experiences of 1992 Hospitalfield students Susan Forsyth, née McMahon (b.1972), and Claire Ashley, née Broadfoot (b.1971), who received advice, guidance and encouragement from SAIC faculty members Susan Kraut and Martin Prekop. Ever since Forsyth's enrolment at Edinburgh College of Art, she had known that she wanted to be a landscape painter. Participating in the Scheme was, therefore, conducive to the practice she wanted to pursue. It was also an opportunity to paint where

FIG. 5.8

Gwen Hardie, Self Portrait in Mirror, *1982*

gouache paint, 45.7 x 38 cm / private collection / / image courtesy of the artist, 2017

one of her artistic heroes, Joan Eardley, had painted. Forsyth recalled that, once at Hospitalfield, Kraut and Prekop encouraged her to 'try and be more experimental' and to challenge herself to 'find a subject that was less about your drawing skills and less about form'.[21] Responding to the light and landscape of Arbroath, Forsyth worked to capture the formlessness of the sky (fig. 5.9). The maturation of her interest in, and skill with capturing, a sense of the endlessly moving forces of nature is evident in Forsyth's later work, which focuses on the ever-changing character of the sea.

For Claire Ashley, the opportunity to interact with the American artists in residence influenced her future direction in both art and life. With the support of Kraut and Prekop, she began creating assemblages that tested the boundaries of painting and sculpture. When reflecting upon this experience, Ashley concluded that it 'was the first significant step in my twenty years of figuring out how to use the colour and material of painting without actually making paintings'.[22] After her final year at Gray's School of Art, Ashley went on to complete a postgraduate degree at the SAIC, where she became a Professor of Contemporary Practices of Drawing and Painting. In her later work, brightly painted surfaces are inflated to created mass, form and a sense of

FROM STUDENT TO ARTIST IN RESIDENCE

Alexander Fraser: student in 1961; artist in residence in 1977 and 1979
'[As an artist in residence] I think you had to be careful not to teach because the students were already identified as talented. I just tried to take an interest in what they were doing individually. There were twelve of them; some did minimal sort of pictures, which didn't occur when I was a student. I think, from reflection, that twelve was too many. It was good that they all got the opportunity to work there, but I think there was something really special about a smaller group.'[23]

Joe McIntyre: student in 1964; artist in residence in 1979
'[In 1964] I was doing quite a lot of landscape work. We were a very competitive group, talking at night about when we would get up and paint in the morning. As a teacher [in 1979], it was good because I was able to relate to the students quite well. We used to go out on trips down to the harbour and did a lot of drawings and paintings there. And I would line up all their work around the wall in the room and we'd talk about what they'd done and we enjoyed that. So they were in competition with each other to see who could get the best painting done.'[24]

Frances Walker: student in 1952; artist in residence in 1983
'When I went back as a visiting artist, I really enjoyed it. I was able not only to get on and do my own work, but I was able to talk to the students, a very lively, interesting mixed bunch of students. Perhaps, already, they were pursuing their own visions. Using the time and space of living and working at Hospitalfield to explore ideas that had already begun to develop was a bit different to being reactive to the landscape, which possibly is what people of my era got out of it. The student of the early eighties saw it in a different way; they were already into individual mind-sets and ways of working. I mean students tend to reflect the opportunities they get, reflect who they are, reflect what's round about them. You're of your time.'[25]

FIG. 5.9
Susan Forsyth, Cloud study, *1992*

oil on canvas, 152 x 122 cm / location unknown / © Susan Forsyth, all rights reserved / image courtesy of the artist, 2017

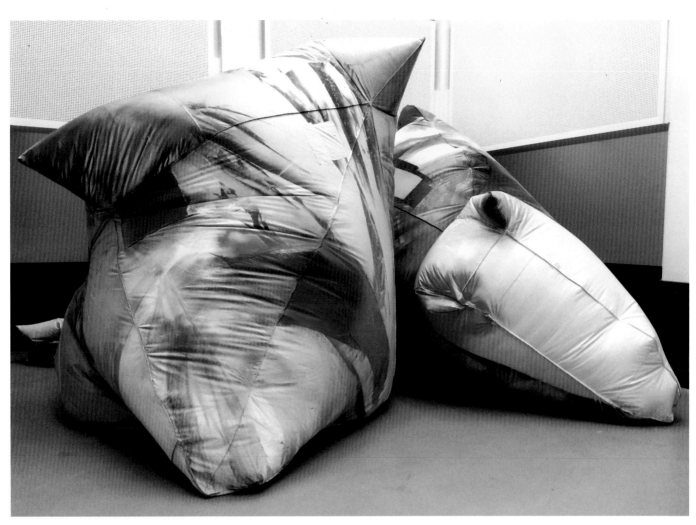

FIG. 5.10
Claire Ashley, The Tasteless Hunk Twins, *2015*

character. Through their use in performance art or installations in galleries or outdoors, Ashley's painted sculptural forms take on new life and meaning in relation to their surroundings.[26] In hindsight, these works can be interpreted as manifestations of the type of multi-disciplinary practice Ashley began at Hospitalfield.

The trajectories of the development of Forsyth's and Ashley's artistic pursuits are reflective of two types of co-existing modes of practice prevalent within Scottish art at the end of the twentieth century. Forsyth's passion for painting and use of imagery based on the visual world can be contextualised as a descendant of the Scottish painting tradition. This tradition was continually cultivated by the art colleges' curricula and the opportunities the Scheme offered to students of drawing and painting.

From this generation emerged artists with a wide range of styles and approaches. Painters like Derrick Guild and Angus McEwan continually employ precision and clarity, whereas Joseph Urie's figurative work is gestural and expressive. While artists such as these explore the representational, others ventured into abstraction with equally diverse styles, from the bold canvases of Andrew Stenhouse to the refined meditative paintings of Callum Innes.[27] In different ways, the work of these artists and their contemporaries has

FIG. 5.11

James Cowie, Set Square

oil on canvas, 62 x 74 cm / University of Aberdeen, Aberdeen (bequeathed by Eric Linklater, 1976)
© the artist's estate, all rights reserved / image courtesy of the University of Aberdeen, 2017

FIG. 5.12

Susan Kraut, Scottish Still Life, V, *1994*

THE LANDSCAPE AND STUDIO AT HOSPITALFIELD: A SOURCE OF INSPIRATION FOR GENERATIONS

The still-life compositions painted by James Cowie during his time as Warden (1937–48) are some of his most evocative works. In his painting Set Square, *the combination of objects — which harks back to Classical art — set against a view of a contemporary landscape, creates a dialogue between past and present, which is imbued with the eerie silence of the suggestion of unseen human presence.*

Almost half a century after Cowie left the studios, the American painter Susan Kraut (b.1945) arrived as artist in residence for a session of the summer of 1992. As windows had been, and continue to be, a motif within Kraut's work, she responded to this same source material by painting studies of everyday objects placed before views to the landscape beyond. These studies were later used to create full-scale oil paintings, such as the 1994 Scottish Still Life, V.

Although Kraut was unaware of Cowie's work at the time, there are striking similarities between the paintings both artists produced. Each painter chose to treat their subjects of still-life and landscape with crisp rendering and a cool palette that reflected the northern light they observed. In addition, Kraut viewed windows 'as a metaphor for painting itself; a framed, selected view of a segment of the world we inhabit',[28] while the repetition of 'frames' in Cowie's Set Square *— from the window, to the work on paper, to the pane of glass — similarly introduced this visual play of pictures within a picture. Such similarities can not only be attributed to the shared conditions in which the artists were working, decades apart, but the intersecting interest in representational painting that emphasised composition and the atmosphere of place within the artists' individual practices. The unknowing parallels between the works highlights the rich source material that Hospitalfield provided and illustrates the process of reinventing motifs and ideas, which keeps the painting tradition vibrant and relevant.*

Susan Kraut is an Adjunct Professor, Painting and Drawing Department, and Chair of the Post-Baccalaureate Program at SAIC. As a painter, she remains fascinated by the stillness and intimacy of interior spaces.

continued to reinvent and reconsider the process and possibilities of painting.

In contrast, artists like Ashley, whose work melds painting, sculpture, installation and performance, have contributed to building the type of multi-disciplinary practice prevalent within twenty-first-century contemporary art. At the end of the twentieth century, this dynamic was only starting to assert its significance in Scotland. From the late 1970s onwards, the art colleges began to evaluate and expand their offerings. The impact of these changes is, perhaps, best illustrated by the formation of Glasgow School of Art's Environmental Art Department.[29] These changes were also felt at Hospitalfield, with the revised 1980 Scheme enabling 'students of the visual arts',[30] rather than just students of drawing and painting, to participate. While, in actuality, few students from other disciplines attended, this did not prevent the drawing and painting students from experimenting with sculpture, performance art and installation.[31] For students like Wendy McMurdo, Donald Urquhart, Kristin Mojsiewicz, Jane Benson and Cordelia Underhill, Hospitalfield offered an opportunity for the germination of practices which would develop into the type of malleable cross-disciplinary approaches that add to today's diverse spectrum of contemporary art.[32]

Changes in Scottish art culture presented new challenges and opportunities for the Scottish art colleges and Hospitalfield as the twentieth century drew to a close, but these institutions would no longer be adapting to the shifting artistic climate in tandem. In response to a variety of ideological and financial factors, the Patrick Allan-Fraser Trust Scheme came to a conclusion in 1994.

Although the nearly sixty-year-old arrangement with the four Scottish art colleges reached its conclusion, Hospitalfield's engagement with the arts continued. Organisational changes led to Payne ceasing to be the Warden of the Scheme and, instead, assuming a role as Director of Hospitalfield Arts, which he held until his retirement in 2012. In several ways, the period from 1994 to 2012 under Payne's direction was comparable to the eleven years of planning prior to opening the Allan-Fraser Art College and the seven years between the closure of the College and the formation of the Patrick Allan-Fraser Trust Scheme. It was a time of reassessment from which a new mission and governance structure eventually emerged. During this period, as from 1890–1901 and 1928–35, Hospitalfield's doors were not closed completely. Several residencies were established through partnerships with arts organisations such as the Royal Scottish Academy, the Royal Scottish Society of Painters in Watercolour, the Royal Overseas League and the European ResArtis network. In addition, through collaboration with Dundee Contemporary Arts, the nineteenth-century dog kennels were renovated to open as the Kinpurnie Print Studio in 2011.

Hospitalfield also found supporters in those who had participated in its programmes throughout the twentieth century as well as in the community. In 2002, the Hospitalfield Alumni Association was formed, providing an opportunity for former participants to reconnect with one another, renew their connection with Hospitalfield and support its future endeavours. The Friends

MAE MCKENZIE SMITH, CHAIR OF THE HOSPITALFIELD ALUMNI ASSOCIATION

Mae McKenzie Smith, née Fotheringham (b.1937), was selected to attend Hospitalfield in 1958 from Glasgow School of Art. She afterwards devoted her energies to the education of aspiring young artists in schools in the northeast of Scotland, while continuing her own practice. Hospitalfield has always held artistic and personal significance for McKenzie Smith. Her belief in its pervasive importance for artists in Scotland throughout the twentieth century motivated her to found the Hospitalfield Alumni Association:

'I became very aware when I met people who suddenly revealed they'd been to Hospitalfield; mention the name and their eyes lit up. They said, 'Oh! It was wonderful. It was so important in my life.' I also became aware that perhaps we could form some kind of alumni association that could be helpful in continuing an association with the place and fulfil some useful purposes. I then put an advertisement into the Royal Scottish Academy catalogue and asked people to contact if they were interested and I got a huge response. We had a first tentative meeting in 2002 to see if this was feasible and got a lot of interest and a lot of support. Hospitalfield was an important asset to twentieth-century Scottish art and that history should not be lost. Of course change is necessary as the world moves on and I'm very excited at what is happening at Hospitalfield now. I believe Patrick Allan-Fraser would have welcomed the present involvement with the twenty-first-century contemporary movements, being the visionary that he was in the nineteenth century, when he created his generous legacy to the students of the future.'[33]

FIG. 5.13

Alastair MacLennan, Berth an Earth, *21 November 2015*

performance commissioned by Hospitalfield as part of the exhibition project, 'CONTINUUM', which focused on the ongoing ripples of influence created by individuals who had studied and taught at Hospitalfield and became artist/teachers elsewhere, 12 November–12 December 2015 / photograph © Louise Coupar, courtesy of Hospitalfield, 2017

ALASTAIR MACLENNAN ON RETURNING TO HOSPITALFIELD

In 2015, Hospitalfield commissioned Berth an Earth, *a performance by Alastair MacLennan (b.1943) that coincided with the exhibition project, 'CONTINUUM', which focused on the ongoing ripples of influence created by individuals who had studied and taught at Hospitalfield and became artist/teachers elsewhere. It had been fifty years since MacLennan had been to Hospitalfield as a student selected to attend the Patrick Allan-Fraser Trust Scheme from Dundee College of Art. His pursuit of art led him from Scotland to the USA and Canada and, finally, to Northern Ireland, where he has lived and worked for the past forty years. In this time, his practice developed in form from drawing and painting to performance art. At the start of* Berth an Earth, *MacLennan encouraged those gathered to consider 'Same Difference'. His reflections on his experiences in 1965 and his return in 2015 can also be considered in terms of the conceptual framework of these words:*

'It was such an enabling context. I'll never forget it. It was something about the generosity of spirit among the young artists who had been at the art schools in Dundee, Edinburgh, Aberdeen and Glasgow, basically helping each other. I was doing academic painting and I suppose people might think performance is so different from that, it seems like a break, but I see the creativity of it more like water: it can be ice, it can be liquid, it can be steam, but its essence, the core principle, remains the same, but its physical articulation is affected by climatic, geographic, other circumstances. I suppose one concern I had, if I had a concern about coming back to do a performance, was if some of the people I was a student with would be horrified at what I'm doing now because it looks so different, but I just see it as something that's naturally evolved from one physical state to another.'[34]

of Hospitalfield was then formed in 2009 to support the preservation of Hospitalfield's history and its continuance as an institution for the arts.

Since 2012, Hospitalfield, under the direction of Lucy Byatt, has found a twenty-first-century vision with a programme of residencies and events that encourage the development of a new generation of artists and enable the public to enjoy Hospitalfield's unique blend of the historic and the contemporary. An ambitious redevelopment plan has also been put in place to conserve the heritage aspects of Hospitalfield House and its collections as well as create new on-site resources for the future.

Not only was Hospitalfield working to make its site more conducive to the enjoyment and education of current and future generations, it was also making international connections. Partnering with artist Graham Fagen, Hospitalfield curated Scotland's 2015 entry to the Venice Biennale, and was first to host this dynamic installation when it returned to Scotland the following year.

Conclusion

There is unbridled imagination and creative feeling in the words of Charles Robert Swift (right), written as he reflected on the place that gave him the foundation for his future career as an artist. They are, in one sense, a tribute to this site of personal significance. They also capture the essence of what made Hospitalfield a germinator of creative endeavour for over one hundred years. Lastly, they are an invitation to all to experience this setting and find inspiration.

Throughout the twentieth century Hospitalfield played a highly significant role in Scottish art education. Both the Allan-Fraser Art College and the Patrick Allan-Fraser Trust Scheme provided unique learning opportunities for their students not available elsewhere in Scotland at the time. The community of artists that these programmes brought together led to heated debates, aesthetic experimentation, ideological questioning and formative friendships. This occurred within the setting of Hospitalfield House with its surrounding agricultural fields and nearby Arbroath harbour, all of which provided stimulating subject matter for artwork. In addition to these, perhaps one of the most precious gifts Hospitalfield bestowed was time — time to experiment with new ways of working or delve into a deepening of artistic practice.

The community, setting and time that Hospitalfield provided was influential to the work and careers of hundreds of artists, both at the time and in the years to follow. For many, the relationships formed at Hospitalfield proved lasting and transformative. Furthermore, as Hospitalfield students became teachers who, in turn, sent their students to Hospitalfield, these connections became multi-generational. For many other Hospitalfield students, learning how to gather visual material and paint *en plein air* were techniques they would return to throughout their careers and, for some, continues to inform the basis of their contemporary work. For others still, the time to work on one's own encouraged the creation of innovative bodies of work as well as the beginnings of ideas that would carry on unfolding and evolving. When the impacts that the Hospitalfield experience had on individual participants are considered beside one another, its significance as a force within the development of art in Scotland and beyond is revealed.

Evidence of this significance is found in the artworks within public and private collections, whose style, subject or even existence is due to the influence that the Hospitalfield experience had upon its participants. Further support exists in the archival records of Hospitalfield and those institutions involved in its governance, which testify not only to the number of students who engaged with its programmes, but also to the formative quality of their experiences. Lastly, oral history interviews record the meanings that artists themselves attribute to their Hospitalfield experiences. Together, these images, archival records and interviews enable Hospitalfield's place in the history of Scottish art, once uncertain and intangible, to become articulated and recognised.

Looking back on twentieth-century Hospitalfield from the twenty-first century, its effects spring from distinct, but related, facets. It was place: an estate with a Victorian manor house built on centuries-old foundations located outside the town centre of Arbroath and within ample grounds. It was an institution: a trust whose mission changed from that of a philanthropic art college to a Scheme that became central to the system of art education by enrolling students from Scotland's art schools. It was a time: the duration of

'Look down on the charming embowered pathway directing the eye to a background of densely wooded scenery such as will inspire the poetic mind with a vision of the soul of things, and stimulate the artist's moulding skill to building up the structures with intense form, grasped from the GREAT CREATIVE MIND beyond the senses, and so catching their true environment. Here, away from the hot and dusty highway, one may recruit mental stability and forget the confusion and dizzy turmoil of everyday life … It leaves us with a sensation of restfulness, an everlasting impression of peace and pure air.'[1]
CHARLES ROBERT SWIFT

a few weeks, the summer months or several years during which an artist worked within a community of peers in the Arbroath locale. In a more ephemeral way, it was a force of influence: changing in specificity and longevity of impact from artist to artist depending on their receptivity and inclination. Through this influence Hospitalfield's twentieth-century legacy continues into the twenty-first century within the contemporary practices of the artists to whom the Hospitalfield experience was so important In this way, twentieth-century Hospitalfield remains an essential part of the continuation of Scotland's vibrant tradition of painting.

When these facets of twentieth-century Hospitalfield are compared with Hospitalfield as it exists in the twenty-first century, many differences can be found. Although it has stayed in the same location, the House now shares a closer proximity with the residential sprawl of Arbroath, a town whose economy is no longer based on fishing and agriculture. As an institution, its mission is broader, engaging with artists, makers, scholars and all those curious about its history and contemporary programmes. The time that participants spend actually engaged with its residencies, exhibitions and projects is, generally, more condensed. Although evidence of its immediate impact on the work and thinking of its participants can be seen, the full extent of the legacy of twenty-first-century Hospitalfield will only be known in some years to come.

Although, in many ways, the Hospitalfield of today bears little resemblance to the bequest of Patrick Allan-Fraser which ushered in its twentieth-century purpose, change has been a constant of the site's history. Differences between Allan-Fraser's bequest and its realisation emerged almost as soon as his appointed Trustees began to bring art-school plans to life. Since then, the mission of Hospitalfield has continued to be shaped by the diverse perspectives of its leaders as well as responding and adapting to changes in Scottish visual art, art education and culture. The specifics of Hospitalfield's characteristics in the twenty-first century have developed in ways that Patrick Allan-Fraser would never have been able to anticipate, yet the more fundamental intentions of his bequest remain. Through each incarnation of its art-educational programming, Hospitalfield has been a place of learning, exchange and inspiration that has supported artistic development.

Today, Hospitalfield, with its distinctive qualities and atmosphere, continues to be a site for the cultivation of art and artists. In this way, it renews Patrick Allan-Fraser's vision, enabling Hospitalfield to continue to be relevant and significant to the development of Scottish art.

Notes

ABBREVIATIONS

ARE Association of the Royal Society of Painter Etchers
ARSA Associate of the Royal Scottish Academy
CBE Commander of the Order of the British Empire
CH Order of the Companions of Honour
DJCAD Duncan of Jordanstone College of Art and Design, formerly Dundee College of Art
ECA Edinburgh College of Art
FRSA Fellow of the Royal Society of Arts
FRSE Fellow of the Royal Society of Edinburgh
GSA Glasgow School of Art
HFRIAS Honorary Fellow of the Royal Incorporation of Architects in Scotland
HRA Honorary Royal Academician
HRHA Honorary Royal Hibernian Academician
HRSA Honorary Royal Scottish Academician
LLD Doctor of Laws
MBE Most Excellent Order of the British Empire
NS National Society of Painters, Sculptors and Engravers
OBE Officer Order of the British Empire
OSA Ontario Society of Artists
PRSA President of the Royal Scottish Academy of Art and Architecture
PPRSA Past President of the Royal Scottish Academy of Art and Architecture
PPRSW Past President of the Royal Scottish Society of Painters in Watercolour
RA Royal Academy
RBA Royal Society of British Artists
RCA Royal Canadian Academy of Arts
RDI Royal Designer for Industry
RGI Royal Glasgow Institute
RHA Royal Hibernian Academy
RI Royal Institute of Painters in Water Colours
ROI Royal Institute of Oil Painters
RP Royal Society of Portrait Painters
RSA Royal Scottish Academy
RSW Royal Scottish Society of Painters in Watercolour
RWA Royal West of England Academy
SED Scottish Education Department

INTRODUCTION

1. Charles Robert Swift, *Hospitalfield: The Home of the Antiquary* (St Albans, 1952), pp. 9, 16.
2. A list detailing participants of the Allan-Fraser Art College and Patrick Allan-Fraser Trust Scheme appears at the back of the book. This is the first published list of this kind and has been compiled through various archival and oral sources. Dates, names and art college affiliations have been cross-referenced when possible.

1. A NEW VISION FOR HOSPITALFIELD

1. Summation informed by: John Gifford, *The Buildings of Scotland: Dundee and Angus* (Yale University Press, 2012); A.H. Millar, 'Hospitalfield: A Proposed College for Artists', *Art Journal* (1896), pp. 246–8; William Payne, *Hospitalfield* (The Trustees of the National Galleries of Scotland, 1990); James Rhynd,

'Hospitalfield: "A Home of Ancient Peace"', *The Scots Magazine* (November 1947), pp. 93–100; Alec Sturrock, 'Patrick Allan-Fraser of Hospitalfield', *Scottish Field*, vol. XCVII, no. 555 (1949), pp. 28–30; Charles Robert Swift, *Hospitalfield: The Home of the Antiquary* (St Albans, 1952).
2. This was a school of art and design run by the Board of Trustees for the Encouragement of Manufacturers in Scotland.
3. Biographical information about Patrick Allan-Fraser informed and cross-referenced from a variety of sources, primarily: Lindsay Errington, *Master Class: Robert Scott Lauder and His Pupils* (National Galleries of Scotland, 1983); George Hay, ed., *The Book of Hospitalfield: Memorial of Patrick Allan-Fraser HRSA of Hospitalfield* (privately printed for the Hospitalfield Trust, 1894); Payne, *Hospitalfield*.
4. Sir Walter Scott, *The Antiquary* (Everyman's Library, 1929), p. 28.
5. Gifford, *The Buildings of Scotland: Dundee and Angus*, p. 337.
6. Hay, ed., *The Book of Hospitalfield*, p. xxv.
7. Rhynd, 'Hospitalfield', p. 96.
8. Rhynd, 'Hospitalfield', p. 96.
9. Millar, 'Hospitalfield', p. 247.
10. 'A New Scottish Art College', *The Graphic* (1902), p. 236.
11. Payne, *Hospitalfield*, pp. 7–8.
12. Sturrock, 'Patrick Allan-Fraser of Hospitalfield', p. 29.
13. 'Death of Mr. Patrick Allan-Fraser of Hospitafield', *The Dundee Courier & Argus*, 18 September 1890.
14. Patrick Allan-Fraser, *An Unpopular View of Our Times* (Myles Macphail, 1861), p. 300.
15. Facts regarding the artist/craftsmen and their work at Hospitalfield informed by Hay, ed., *The Book of Hospitalfield*, pp. xxv–xxvii.
16. Allan-Fraser is classified as an amateur painter in Esme Gordon, *The Royal Scottish Academy of Painting, Sculpture & Architecture: 1826–1976* (Charles Skilton Ltd, 1976), p. 30, but as a professional in James L. Caw, *Scottish Painting Past and Present: 1620–1908* (Kingsmead Reprints, 1975), p. 226. Allan-Fraser is referred to as an artist and amateur architect and Hospitalfield and the Mortuary Chapel contextualised as examples of Victorian fantasy in Gifford, *The Buildings of Scotland: Dundee and Angus*, pp. 46–7, 320, 337–8. Allan-Fraser's taste in architecture is heavily criticised in Ian Finlay, *The Story of Scots Architecture* (Douglas & Foulis, 1951), pp. 50–56. All sources mentioned confirm his status as a patron of the arts.
17. The position of Honorary Royal Scottish Academician is 'the highest compliment the Royal Scottish Academy has to bestow' – Gordon, *The Royal Scottish Academy of Painting, Sculpture & Architecture*, p. 30.
18. 'Death of Mr. Patrick Allan Fraser of Hospitalfield'.
19. Rhynd, 'Hospitalfield', p. 95.
20. Sarah Carr-Gomm, *Dictionary of Symbols in Art* (Duncan Baird Publishers, 2000), p. 51.
21. Summary informed by Allan-Fraser, 'Deed of Settlement and Mortification', Hay, ed., *The Book of Hospitalfield*, pp. 1–33.
22. Patrick Allan-Fraser, 'Deed of Settlement and Mortification', Hay, ed., *The Book of Hospitalfield*, p. 1.
23. Hay alludes to this in *The Book of Hospitalfield* and a similar characterisation of Allan-Fraser appears in

'Mr. Gladstone's Visit to Blackcraig', *The Dundee Courier & Argus*, 5 August 1893: 'So particular was the proprietor when it was being built that various parts of it, after being built, were taken down if the effect did not please his artist eye, and built in a more suitable fashion.'
24. Jim Fiddes and Ross Hayworth, eds, *Gray's 120* (The Robert Gordon University, 2005).
25. For more about the evolution of art education in Dundee, see: Matthew Jarron, *Independent and Individualist* (Abertay Historical Society, 2015), pp. 155–9.
26. For examples see: 'Will of the Late Mr. Patrick Allan-Fraser of Hospitalfield: Important Public Bequest', *The Glasgow Herald*, 23 September 1890; 'Mr Allan Fraser's Will: Remarkable Bequest', *The Dundee Courier & Argus*, 23 September 1890.
27. Millar, 'Hospitalfield', p. 248.

2. FROM CREATION TO COLLAPSE

1. The original Trustees included: William Calder Marshall, RA, London; James Drummond, RSA, Edinburgh; John Hutchinson, RSA, Edinburgh; Alexander Hay Milne of Woodhill; William Blair-Imrie of Lunan; John Guthrie Smith, Sheriff of Aberdeen and Kincardine; John Clerk Brodie of Idvies, Forfarshire; William Kid MacDonald, Town Clerk, Arbroath; and Robert Whyte, Solicitor and Bank Agent, Forfar. Trustees dealt with the logistical concerns of paying death duties, settling outstanding debts and coming to terms with how the Hospitalfield estate could support the philanthropic school. While the art school was in a phase of planning, Hospitalfield was still contributing to the cultural milieu. During the summer, its galleries were opened for visitors to enjoy the collections and architecture. Although the majority of these came from Arbroath and the surrounding towns and cities, visitors also travelled from as far as Edinburgh, London and even South Africa.
2. This text refers to the art school at Hospitalfield as the Allan-Fraser Art College because that is the name that appears in the Minutes of the Trustees. Other articles and entries in books refer to the same institution with slightly varying names and frequently misspell the name of Patrick Allan-Fraser.
3. James L. Caw, *Scottish Painting Past and Present: 1620–1908* (Kingsmead Reprints, 1975), p. 226.
4. For examples see: 'Gray's School of Art, Aberdeen', *Aberdeen Weekly Journal*, 20 December 1886; *Technical Institute, Dundee: Syllabus of Science and Art Classes 1893–1894* (John Leng & Co., 1892), p. 15; George Rawson, 'The Renfrew Street Panopticon: Francis Newbery and the Reinvention of [the] Glasgow School of Art', Ray McKenzie, ed., *The Flower and the Green Leaf* (Luath Press Ltd, 2009), p. 20.
5. M.H. Spielmann, 'To Those Whom It May Concern: The New Free Art University', *The Magazine of Art* (1901), p. 507.
6. Charles Robert Swift was one of the first eight students to be accepted into the College in 1901. Swift made a career in illustration and along with *Hospitalfield: The Home of the Antiquary*, wrote, illustrated and published several books about local landmarks and points of interest.

7. Charles Robert Swift, *Hospitalfield: The Home of the Antiquary* (St Albans, 1952), p. 9.

8. Copy Letter from Mr Henry W. Daniel, dated 27 February 1928, p. 9, Hospitalfield Box 2/2, Royal Scottish Academy Archives, Edinburgh.

9. Paragraph informed by: Austin Cooper, *Making a Poster* (The Studio Ltd, 1938); Paul Rennie, *Modern British Posters* (Black Dog Publishing, 2010); Grant M. Waters, *Dictionary of British Artists: Working 1900–1950* (Eastbourne Fine Art, 1975), p. 75; 'Austin Cooper: 1890–1964', *Tate* online, www.tate.org.uk/art/artists/austin-cooper-939, accessed 26 July 2016; 'Artist-Austin Cooper', *London Transport Museum* online, 2010, www.ltmcollection.org/posters/artist/artist.html?IXartist=Austin+Cooper, accessed 26 July 2016.

10. 'Allan Fraser Art College: Report by the Governor for Session 1905–1906', p. 527, *Minute Book: Hospitalfield Trust 1895–1907*, Hospitalfield, Arbroath.

11. 'Allan Fraser Art College: Report by the Governor for Session 1905–1906', p. 527, *Minute Book: Hospitalfield Trust 1895–1907*, Hospitalfield, Arbroath.

12. 'Novel Entertainment at Hospitalfield', *The Scotsman*, 20 February 1909, p. 12.

13. Portions of his unpublished accounts appear in Neville Jason and Lisa Thompson-Pharoah, *The Sculpture of Frank Dobson* (The Henry Moore Foundation, 1994), pp. 17–23.

14. Janice Helland, *Professional Woman Painters in Nineteenth-century Scotland* (Ashgate Publishing, 2000), pp. 18–9, 52, 73.

15. The enrolment lists from 1901 to 1927 included names of only male residential and day students. If any female day students did attend, their names were not recorded. It was not until 1940 that women were allowed to participate in artistic training at Hospitalfield. 'Memo as to Appointment of Students to the Hospitalfield Art College', 1925, pp. 300–5, *Minute Book: Hospitalfield Trust 1921–1936*, Hospitalfield, Arbroath.

16. 'Deed of Settlement and Mortification', George Hay, ed., *The Book of Hospitalfield: Memorial of Patrick Allan-Fraser HRSA of Hospitalfield* (privately printed for the Hospitalfield Trust, 1894), p. 18.

17. Tom Normand, *Portfolio* (Luath Press Ltd, 2013), p. 15.

18. For more about female artists and their educational experiences in Scotland see: Alice Strang, ed., *Modern Scottish Women: Painters & Sculptors 1885–1965* (the Trustees of the National Galleries of Scotland, 2015).

19. 'Allan Fraser Art College: Report by the Governor for Session 1903–1904', p. 453, *Minute Book: Hospitalfield Trust 1895–1907*, Hospitalfield, Arbroath.

20. 'Allan Fraser Art College: Report by the Governor for Session 1903–1904', p. 453, *Minute Book: Hospitalfield Trust 1895–1907*, Hospitalfield, Arbroath.

21. Joanna Soden, 'Tradition, Evolution, Opportunism: The Role of the Royal Scottish Academy in Art Education 1826–1910' (PhD diss., University of Aberdeen, 2006), p. 235.

22. 'Arbroath Art Galleries Closed', *The Observer*, 14 June 1914, p. 8.

23. 'Suffragettes', *The Scotsman*, 27 May 1914.

24. 'Frank Dobson & Bernard Adams' was informed by: Waters, *Dictionary of British Artists: Working 1900–1950*, pp. 3–4; Jason and Thompson-Pharoah, *The Sculpture of Frank Dobson*, p. 22; Sophie Bowness, ed., *Carving Mountains: Modern Stone Sculpture in England 1907–1937* (Kettle's Yard, 1998).

25. Biographical information about the Harcourt family informed by: Charles Baile de Laperrière, ed., *The Royal Scottish Academy Exhibitors: 1826–1990* (Hilmarton Press, 1991), vol. II, p. 231; Grant Longman, *The Herkomer Art School and Subsequent Development: 1901–1918* (E.G. Longman, 1981); David Setford, *Stand by Your Work: Hubert von Herkomer and His Students* (Borough Council, 1983); Waters, *Dictionary of British Artists: Working 1900–1950*, pp. 149–50. 'The Royal Academy, London', *The Scotsman*, 2 May 1903, p. 9.

26. Allan-Fraser foresaw that the students' separation from the art of Scotland's urban centres could be detrimental to keeping abreast of new developments in art. He therefore specified that the students visit exhibitions in Edinburgh and Glasgow annually and that scholars of science and art be brought to Hospitalfield for lectures. The Governors reports to the Trustees reveal their agreement to the benefit of this exposure. 'Deed of Settlement and Mortification', Hay, ed., *The Book of Hospitalfield*, pp. 13–4; 'Allan Fraser Art College: Report by the Governor for Session 1903–1904', p. 454, *Minute Book: Hospitalfield Trust 1895–1907*, Hospitalfield, Arbroath; 'First Main Purpose of the Trust', 7 October 1921, p. 646, *Minute Book: Hospitalfield Trust 1907–1921*, Hospitalfield, Arbroath.

27. 'Advertisement for Adam's Atelier from the Year's Art, 1892', reproduced in Maria Devaney, *Mountain, Meadow, Moss and Moor* (Smith Art Gallery and Museum, 1996).

28. 'Allan Fraser Art College: Report by the Governor for Session 1903–1904', p. 453, *Minute Book: Hospitalfield Trust 1885–1907*, Hospitalfield, Arbroath.

29. Biographical information about John Murray Thomson informed by: E.M. & J. Murray Thomson, *Animals We Know* (T.C. & E.C. Jack Ltd, 1924). See also Charles Baile de Laperrière, ed., *The Royal Scottish Academy Exhibitors: 1826–1990*, vol. IV, pp. 324–6; Waters, *Dictionary of British Artists: Working 1900–1950*, p. 327.

30. Caw, *Scottish Painting Past and Present*, p. 226.

31. For more see George Rawson, '"The Renfrew Street Panopticon": Francis Newbery and the Reinvention of [the] Glasgow School of Art', McKenzie, ed., *The Flower and the Green Leaf*, pp. 17–9.

32. 'Hospitalfield Trust: Report by George Harcourt', 1902, p. 332, *Minute Book: Hospitalfield Trust 1895–1907*, Hospitalfield, Arbroath.

33. This timeline was informed by: Caw, *Scottish Painting Past and Present*; Lindsay Errington, *Master Class: Robert Scott Lauder and His Pupils* (National Galleries of Scotland, 1983); Jim Fiddes and Ross Hayworth, eds, *Gray's 120* (The Robert Gordon University, 2005); Matthew Jarron, *Independent and Individualist* (Abertay Historical Society, 2015); McKenzie, ed., *The Flower and the Green Leaf*; 'Art and History in Glasgow', *Journal of the Scottish Society for Art History*, vol. 12 (2007).

34. Caw, *Scottish Painting Past and Present*, pp. 424–5; G. Frederic Lees, 'The Art of George Harcourt', *The Studio*, vol. LXX (1917), pp. 160–9.

35. The present condition of this painting makes it unsuitable for illustration. There are few surviving examples of student work. Although a College Prospectus stated, 'All works produced by the students while in residence are the property of the Hospitalfield Trustees', there is no documentation to confirm if such works were kept.

36. Lees, 'The Art of George Harcourt', p. 169.

37. The fact that students learned to paint in this way was also referenced in accounts by Frank Dobson, published in Jason and Thompson-Pharoah, *The Sculpture of Frank Dobson*, pp. 18–19.

38. Lees, 'The Art of George Harcourt', p. 169.

George Rawson and Ray McKenzie, 'Art Is the Flower', McKenzie, ed., *The Flower and the Green Leaf*, pp. 65–79.

39. Biographical information about John Hay was informed by: 'Memo as to Appointment of Students to the Hospitalfield Art College', 1925, p. 303, *Minute Book: Hospitalfield Trust 1921–1936*, Hospitalfield, Arbroath; Waters, *Dictionary of British Artists: Working 1900–1950*, p. 155.

40. This paragraph was informed by Alfred Lys Baldry, *Hubert von Herkomer, RA: A Study and a Biography* (George Bell and Sons, 1901); Lee MacCormick Edwards, *Herkomer: A Victorian Artist* (Ashgate Publishing, 1999); Longman, *The Herkomer Art School and Subsequent Development: 1901–1918*; Setford, *Stand by Your Work*.

41. Lys Baldry, *Hubert von Herkomer, RA: A Study and a Biography*, p. 60.

42. Allan Newton Sutherland was a young talent from Aberdeen whose career was cut short when he died in action during the First World War. John Morrison, *Particles of Light* (Robert Gordon University, 2000), p. 35. Evidence of him exhibiting: de Laperrière, ed., *The Royal Scottish Academy Exhibitors: 1826–1990*, p. 281.

43. After his studies Thomas Percival Anderson seems to have returned to his native Yorkshire and become a portrait painter according to 'Memo as to Appointment of Students to the Hospitalfield Art College', 1925, p. 302, *Minute Book: Hospitalfield Trust 1921–1936*, Hospitalfield, Arbroath. Nineteen of his portraits are in the collection of the York Museums Trust. In his unpublished memoirs Frank Dobson speaks of Anderson as a friend with whom he had lively discussion about art, as recorded in Jason and Thompson-Pharoah, *The Sculpture of Frank Dobson*, p. 19.

44. Arnold Mason had a successful artist's career, being elected to the Royal Academy and Royal Society of Portrait Painters. Forty-six of his oil paintings, mainly portraits, are held in UK public collections. Also see: Waters, *Dictionary of British Artists: Working 1900–1950*, p. 226.

45. Lys Baldry, *Hubert von Herkomer*, p. 91.

46. 'Allan Fraser Art College: Report by the Governor for Session 1905–1906', p. 527, *Minute Book: Hospitalfield Trust 1895–1907*, Hospitalfield, Arbroath.

47. After his time at the College, James Bell Anderson went on to study in Paris before settling in Glasgow. There he became best known for his portraits and was elected to the Royal Scottish Academy. Robert Timmis spent the majority of his career as an art teacher at Liverpool School of Art. 'Memo as to Appointment of Students to the Hospitalfield Art College', 1925, p. 303, *Minute Book: Hospitalfield Trust 1921–1936*, Hospitalfield, Arbroath; 'Scottish Artist', *The Scotsman*, 21 November 1938, p. 7; Waters, *Dictionary of British Artists*, p. 10.

48. For references regarding Harcourt see: Lees, 'The Art of George Harcourt', pp. 162, 165; Caw, *Scottish Painting Past and Present*, pp. 424–5; Julian Halsby and Paul Harris, *The Dictionary of Scottish Painters: 1600 to the Present* (Birlinn Ltd, 2010), p. 92. 'The Royal Academy London', *The Scotsman*, 2 May 1903, p. 9.

49. From 1892 to 1906 Munnoch held a variety of teaching roles in Stirling, Kirkcaldy and Elgin, obtained teaching qualifications from the SED and South Kensington, and continued his studies in art at the Royal Institution and Royal Scottish Academy Life School. From the Royal Scottish Academy Life School he received the Chalmer's Bursary for Painting in 1905, the Chalmers-Jervice Prize for Drawing in 1906, and the prestigious Andrew Carnegie Travelling Scholarship in 1907.

50. Letter of recommendation by Charles D. Hodder,

Headmaster of the School of Art, Royal Institution, Edinburgh, 14 October 1898. Copy provided by Hospitalfield.

51. Letter of recommendation by Matthew H.W. Whittest, Art Master at Victoria School of Science and Art, Elgin, 14 January 1904. Copy provided by Hospitalfield.

52. 'Copy of Report by the Governor of the Allan-Fraser Art College', dated October 1924, p. 9, Hospitalfield Box 2/2, Royal Scottish Academy Archives, Edinburgh.

53. The name in the title of the Ramsay original is usually, in fact, given as Anna and not Anne, although over time the Munnoch version has been catalogued as Anne.

54. 'Allan Fraser Art College: Report by the Governor to the Trustees', 8 October 1910, p. 192, *Minute Book: Hospitalfield Trust 1907–1921*, Hospitalfield; 'Report to the Hospitalfield Trust by the Governor of the Allan Fraser Art College', October 1911, pp. 251–2, *Minute Book: Hospitalfield Trust 1907–1921*, Hospitalfield, Arbroath.

55. Paragraph informed by: Joan M. Matthews, *J.B. Souter: 1890–1971* (Perth Museum and Art Gallery, 1990).

56. The Souter image can be found catalogued/referred to as *Man with a Red Hat (Copy after Titian)*.

57. For biographical information about Stanley Horace Gardiner see: 'Stanley Gardiner', *Penlee House Gallery and Museum* online, www.penleehouse.org.uk/artists/stanley-gardiner.html, accessed 26 July 2016; Waters, *Dictionary of British Artists: Working 1900–1950*, p. 124.

58. Jason and Thompson-Pharoah, *The Sculpture of Frank Dobson*, p. 22.

59. For biographical information about Adam Sheriff Scott see: Evelyn de R. McMann, *Royal Canadian Academy of Arts* (University of Toronto Press, 1981), p. 367. 'Adam Sheriff Scott', *TMR Art Gallery* online, www.montroyalartgallery.com/english/ascott.htm, accessed 26 July 2016.

60. For biographical information about Kenneth Forbes see: de R. McMann, *Royal Canadian Academy of Arts*, pp. 128–9. 'Kenneth Forbes', *Canadian Museum of History* online, 2004, http://collections.historymuseum.ca/public/pages/cmccpublic/emupublic/Display.php?irn=1016529&lang=0, accessed 26 July 2016.

61. 'Memo as to Appointment of Students to the Hospitalfield Art College', 1925, pp. 300–5, *Minute Book: Hospitalfield Trust 1921–1936*, Hospitalfield, Arbroath. Some of these can also be found on the Commonwealth War Graves Commission database at www.cwgc.org/find-war-dead.aspx.

62. Based on material from a transcription of a lecture, 'The Girl in "The Chinese Coat": John Munnoch 1879–1915', written and delivered by Elma Lindsay as part of Stirling Stories 2006.

63. For more on John Munnoch see Patricia R. Andrew, *A Chasm in Time* (Birlinn, 2014), p. 93.

64. 'Report to the Hospitalfield Trust by the Governor of the Allan-Fraser Art College', 15 October 1915, pp. 499–500, *Minute Book: Hospitalfield Trust 1907–1921*, Hospitalfield, Arbroath.

65. 'Report to the Hospitalfield Trust by the Governor of the Allan-Fraser Art College', 15 October 1915, pp. 499–500, *Minute Book: Hospitalfield Trust 1907–1921*, Hospitalfield, Arbroath.

66. Biographical information about Henry Daniel informed by: de Laperriere, ed., *The Royal Scottish Academy Exhibitors: 1826–1990*, p. 391; 'Dundee Artists' Work at the Royal Academy', *Evening Telegraph*, 7 May 1935.

67. 'Report by Mr. Henry Daniel, Governor', 22 October 1927, p. 404, *Minute Book Hospitalfield Trust: 1921–1936*, Hospitalfield, Arbroath.

68. 'Dundee Artists' Work at the Royal Academy', *Evening Telegraph*, 7 May 1935.

69. Charles Christie Ruxton was one of the only known natives of Arbroath to participate in the College and was the last student in attendance under Daniel. He later completed his studies at Dundee College of Technology and School of Art.

70. For more, see *Joseph Webb: 1908–1962* (D&F Galleries, 1968).

71. Timeline informed by archival material in Hospitalfield Box 2/2, Royal Scottish Academy Archives, Edinburgh.

72. Profits and losses began to fluctuate between £100 and £500 per year from 1911 to 1913 and the deficit continually grew between £100 and £2,400 per year from 1914 to 1928. 'Artists: Angus Man's Scheme: Inadequacy of Income', *The Scotsman*, 17 July 1929, p. 16.

73. Correspondence from George Washington Browne, PRSA, to Messrs. J.&W. Macdonald, Solicitors, Arbroath, 'Hospitalfield Trust', 7 October 1924, Hospitalfield Box 2/2, Royal Scottish Academy Archives, Edinburgh.

74. It was through Paterson's recommendation that Henry Daniel was appointed and also Paterson who suggested two students from Edinburgh College of Art be admitted to Hospitalfield to continue their education. 'Special Meeting of the Trustees', 14 January 1927, p. 358, *Minute Book Hospitalfield Trust: 1921–1936*, Hospitalfield, Arbroath; 'Report by Mr. Henry Daniel, Governor', 22 October 1927, p. 404, *Minute Book Hospitalfield Trust: 1921–1936*, Hospitalfield, Arbroath.

75. Roger Billcliffe, *The Glasgow Boys* (John Murray Publishers Ltd, 1985), p. 301.

76. James Paterson, 'A Note on Nationality in Art', *The Scottish Art Review*, vol. 1, no. 3 (1888), p. 89.

77. Copy of Report by the Governor of the Allan-Fraser Art College, October 1924, Hospitalfield Box 2/2, Royal Scottish Academy Archives, Edinburgh.

78. Copy of letter from Mr Henry W. Daniel, 27 February 1928, p. 6, Hospitalfield Box 2/2, Royal Scottish Academy Archives, Edinburgh.

79. John A. Brown quoted in 'Burns' Anniversary', *The Isle of Man Times and General Advertiser*, 31 January 1891, p. 3.

80. Patrick Allan-Fraser, 'Deed of Settlement and Mortification', Hay, ed., *The Book of Hospitalfield*, p. 5.

3. THE ERA OF ARTIST-WARDENS

1. Section 26, p. 11, 'Patrick Allan-Fraser Trust Scheme, 1935: At the Court at Buckingham Palace, the 30th Day of April, 1936', Box 39, Archives & Collections Centre, Glasgow School of Art, Glasgow.

2. Summary is informed by 'Patrick Allan-Fraser Trust Scheme, 1935: At the Court at Buckingham Palace, the 30th day of April, 1936' etc: 'It should be noted that the financial instability that caused the institutional changesalso made continuing the College's philanthropic mission impossible. Vestiges of philanthropy remained, as it was, as in 'the power of the governing body to admit free of charge or at a modified charge and to pay the travelling expenses of any student who satisfies them that he could not from his own resources provide.' The Scheme also instructed that if additional funds remained, bursaries could be granted to young people from Arbroath to pursue training at one of the four Scottish art colleges.

3. Many of the arguments made in this chapter are expanded upon in Peggy Beardmore's 2016 PhD dissertation, 'The Significance of Hospitalfield in the Development of 20th-century Scottish Art: The Artwork and Influence of James Cowie and Ian Fleming', University of Aberdeen.

4. Although two of these are 'schools' of art and two are 'colleges' of art, for brevity, they will be referred to throughout the text as the four Scottish art colleges.

5. 'Art Interests: A Landscape School', *The Scotsman*, 22 May 1934, p. 11.

6. Despite being governed by Trustees representing four co-educational art colleges, when the Scheme began only male students were admitted. This incongruity reflected the continued existence of gender inequality in terms of artistic opportunity and the separate societal expectations for men and women.

7. For examples see: William Hardie, *Scottish Painting: 1837–Present*, 3rd ed. (Waverley Books, 2010), pp. 147–9, 196; Keith Hartley, *Scottish Art since 1900* (Lund Humphries, 1989), pp. 22–4, 125, 132–3; Murdo Macdonald, *Scottish Art* (Thames & Hudson, 2000), pp. 173–6; Alison Brown, *Ian Fleming: A Major Retrospective Exhibition* (Aberdeen Art Gallery and Museum, 1996); Richard Calvocaressi, *James Cowie* (Scottish National Gallery of Modern Art, 1979); Duncan Macmillan, *Scottish Art: 1460–2000* (Mainstream Publishing, 2nd ed., 2000), pp. 340–6, 360–3; Cordelia Oliver, *James Cowie* (Edinburgh University Press, 1980); Cordelia Oliver, *James Cowie: The Artist at Work* (Scottish Arts Council, 1981).

8. The article by Bill Connon, 'James Cowie, Painter', *Leopard Magazine*, July/August 2002, identifies the Needle's E'e as the cave whose opening appears in *Evening Star*, and the view from Dickmont's Den as having informed other aspects of the paintings, including the rock formation that appears in the background.

9. Work by Cowie, Sivell, McGlashan and Lamont are compared in W.O. Hutchison, Foreword to *Four Scottish Painters* (The Arts Council of Great Britain, 1948). Connections between Cowie, Baird and McIntosh Patrick are discussed in Macdonald, *Scottish Art*, pp. 174–5. Cowie, McGlashan, Sivell and sculptor Benno Schotz were also founder members of the Glasgow Society of Painters and Sculptors. Macmillan identifies stylistic similarities among this group as well as connections between them and the Edinburgh Group. Macmillan, *Scottish Art: 1460–2000*, pp. 337–8.

10. These connections and identifications were proposed in Richard Calvocaressi, *James Cowie RSA: 1886–1956* (Scottish National Gallery of Modern Art, 1978), p. 6; Macmillan, *Scottish Art: 1460–2000*, p. 346.

11. This identification was made in Oliver, *James Cowie: The Artist at Work*, p. 3.

12. Greater discussions of the meaning and implication of this statement can be found in: Richard Kendall, ed., *Cézanne and Poussin* (Sheffield Academic Press, 1993).

13. James Cowie in Appendix 1 of Calvocaressi, *James Cowie*.

14. Cowie as quoted in 'Modern Art', *The Arbroath Herald*, 12 April 1946.

15. Cowie as quoted in Colin Gibson, *The Scots Magazine*, vol. LV, no. 3 (1951), pp. 182–3.

16. T. Elder Dickson, 'Former Hospitalfield Warden', *The Arbroath Herald*, 23 November 1951.

17. 'An Outdoor School of Painting', 'Art and Artists', *Tate* online, www.tate.org.uk/art/artworks/cowie-an-outdoor-school-of-painting-t03549, accessed 13 February 2018; Waistel Cooper, *Independent* online, 17 February 2003, www.independent.co.uk/news/obituaries/waistel-cooper-36272.html), accessed 13 February 2018.

18. The identity of the female figure lying in the grass is unknown. This same figure appears in Cowie's 1946 painting *Noon*.

19. 'Warden's Report', dated 1944, p. 387, *Minute Book Hospitalfield Trust: 1936–1946*, Hospitalfield, Arbroath.
20. Oliver, *James Cowie: The Artist at Work*, p. 4.
21. Oliver, *James Cowie*, pp. 1, 68.
22. 'Art Exhibition', Arbroath Guide, 18 January 1947.
23. 'Report on Work for Session April to September 1941', p. 237, *Minute Book Hospitalfield Trust: 1936–1946*, Hospitalfield, Arbroath.
24. Adapted from p. 1 of Peggy Beardmore's original transcription of Morris Grassie, interviewed by Peggy Beardmore, 13 March 2014, EI2014.064, Elphinstone Institute, University of Aberdeen, Aberdeen.
25. Page 1 of Peggy Beardmore's original transcription of Morris Grassie, interviewed by Peggy Beardmore, 13 March 2014 etc.
26. The first known Arbroath Art Society was founded in the late nineteenth century, but soon dwindled, during the First World War. In 1946, a new Arbroath Art Society was founded and still continues today.
27. Roger Bristow, *The Last Bohemians* (Sansom & Company, 2010), pp. 31–9.
28. Ruth Christie, correspondence with Peggy Beardmore, April–June 2017.
29. For examples see: Bristow, *The Last Bohemians*, pp. 35–37; Andrew Gibbon Williams and Andrew Brown, *The Bigger Picture: A History of Scottish Art* (BBC Books, 1993), p. 193.
30. Bristow, *The Last Bohemians*, p. 32.
31. The flare's reference to the impending or yet to begin Second World War (the date of the painting is only an estimation) informed by correspondence with the Estate of Alexander Allan, June 2017.
32. Merlin James and David Stephenson, *Ray Howard-Jones: The Elements of Art* (The Rocket Press, 1993).
33. The biographical information and quotation in *Ray Howard-Jones at Hospitalfield* is from James and Stephenson, *Ray Howard-Jones*.
34. 'Hospitalfield Art College: Report', 1947, Hospitalfield Box 1/2, Royal Scottish Academy Archives, Edinburgh.
35. Christopher Andreae, *Joan Eardley* (Lund Humphries, 2013), pp. 52–3; Cordelia Oliver, *Joan Eardley, RSA* (Mainstream Publishing, 1988), pp. 25–6.
36. Fiona Pearson, *Joan Eardley* (National Galleries of Scotland, 2007), p. 16. Excerpt of Joan Eardley letter to Margot Sandeman as recorded in Christopher Andreae, *Joan Eardley* (Lund Humphries, 2013), p. 52.
37. Excerpt from Joan Eardley's letter to her mother, as recorded in Christopher Andreae, *Joan Eardley* (Lund Humphries, 2013), p. 52.
38. Excerpt from Joan Eardley's letter to her mother, as recorded in Andreae, *Joan Eardley*, p. 52.
39. This conclusion is confirmed by Cowie's report to the Trustees: 'Hospitalfield Art College: Report', 1947, Hospitalfield Box 1/2, Royal Scottish Academy Archives, Edinburgh, as well as by Ruth Christie.
40. Adapted from p. 1 of Peggy Beardmore's original transcription of David Lockhart, interviewed by Peggy Beardmore, 28 October 2014, EI2014.084, Elphinstone Institute, University of Aberdeen, Aberdeen.
41. Adapted from p. 1 of Peggy Beardmore's original transcription of David Lockhart, interviewed by Peggy Beardmore, 28 October 2014 etc.
42. Joyce McMillan, 'Obituary: David Lockhart, Artist and Musician', *The Scotsman* online, 10 January 2015, www.scotsman.com/news/obituaries/obituary-david-lockhart-artist-and-musician-1-3656802, accessed 26 July 2016.
43. 'Report on Work at Hospitalfield Art College, 1939', p. 145, *Minute Book Hospitalfield Trust: 1936–1946*, Hospitalfield, Arbroath.
44. 'Warden's Report', 1945, p. 336, *Minute Book Hospitalfield Trust: 1936–1946*, Hospitalfield, Arbroath.
45. Christie, correspondence with Peggy Beardmore, April–June 2017.
46. 'Report on work at Hospitalfield Art College, 1939', p. 145, *Minute Book Hospitalfield Trust: 1936–1946*, Hospitalfield, Arbroath.
47. For more about these artists and female Scottish artists see: Alice Strang, ed., *Modern Scottish Women: Painters & Sculptors 1885–1965* (Trustees of the National Galleries of Scotland, 2015).
48. Letter entitled 'Patrick Allan Fraser Trust' from the Scottish Educational Department, 6 December 1951, File 149, *Hospitalfield Patrick Allan Trust: February 1933–March 1961*, Edinburgh College of Art Archives, the University of Edinburgh, Edinburgh.
49. Adapted from pp. 7–10 of Peggy Beardmore's original transcription of Hugh Robertson, interviewed by Peggy Beardmore, 18 March 2014, EI2014.065, Elphinstone Institute, University of Aberdeen, Aberdeen.
50. Paragraph informed by: Patricia R. Andrew, *A Chasm in Time* (Birlinn, 2014), p. 157; David McClure, 'R. Henderson Blyth (1919–1970)', *Scottish Art Review*, vol. XIII, no. 3 (1972), pp. 21–2; Felix McCulloch, 'Robert Henderson Blyth', *Four Scottish Artists* (The Scottish Committee of the Arts Council of Great Britain, 1964).
51. Paragraph informed by: Andrew, *A Chasm in Time*, pp. 114–6, 152–3; Macmillan, *Scottish Art: 1460–2000*, pp. 361–2.
52. Anne Whyte, ed., *Ian Fleming: Graphic Work* (Peacock Printmakers, 1983), p. 11.
53. Whyte, ed., *Ian Fleming*, p. 11.
54. Ian Fleming on the occasion of the Scottish Gallery's 1987 exhibition of his *Comment Series* appearing in Ian Fleming's artist file at the National Art Library, Victoria and Albert Museum, London.
55. 'Praise from Hospitalfield College Warden', *The Arbroath Herald*, 30 April 1948.
56. The composition and many visual attributes of Arbroath's *St John Preaching in the Wilderness*, of which another similar 1601 version is in the Rheinisches Landesmuseum, Bonn, was derived from Pieter Brueghel the Elder's 1566 *Preaching of St John the Baptist*, in the collection of the Szepmuveszeti Museum, Budapest.
57. Macmillan, *Scottish Art: 1460–2000*, p. 362.
58. Emile Michel and Victoria Charles, *Pieter Brueghel* (Parkstone International, 2012), pp. 16, 38.
59. The idea of immersion in nineteenth-century paintings is discussed at length in: Nina Lübbren, *Rural Artists' Colonies in Europe: 1870–1910* (Manchester University Press, 2001), pp. 98–127.
60. John Morrison, *Painting Labour in Scotland and Europe: 1805–1910* (Ashgate Publishing, 2014), p. 158.
61. It is generally accepted among scholars that the work of Bastien-Lepage influenced the artistic development of Guthrie and others of the Glasgow Boys. For examples see: Roger Billcliffe, *The Glasgow Boys* (John Murray Publishers Ltd, 1985), pp. 37, 81; Morrison, *Painting Labour in Scotland and Europe*, p. 10.
62. Quotation reproduced in Jean Bouret, *The Barbizon School and 19th Century French Landscape Painting* (Thames & Hudson, 1973), p. 29.
63. 'Warden's Report', 1948, p. 80, *Minute Book Hospitalfield Trust: 1947–1961*, Hospitalfield, Arbroath.
64. 'Hospitalfield Art Students "Discover" Arbroath', *The Arbroath Herald*, 22 October 1948, p. 3.
65. George Bruce, *William Burns* (Aberdeen Art Gallery, 1973).
66. The impact of Hospitalfield on the work of Frances Walker is expanded upon in Peggy Beardmore, 'From the Beginning with Frances Walker: An Exploration of Lifelong Practice', *The Journal of the Scottish Society of Art History*, vol. 21 (2016–17), pp. 61–8.
67. Biographical information obtained from conversations and correspondence between Frances Walker and Peggy Beardmore.
68. Adapted from p. 1 of Peggy Beardmore's original transcription of Frances Walker, interviewed by Peggy Beardmore, 24 April 2014, EI2014.067, Elphinstone Institute, University of Aberdeen, Aberdeen.
69. Biographical information and imagery identification in this paragraph obtained from conversations between Morris Grassie and Peggy Beardmore.
70. For more see: Herbert Read, *Contemporary British Art* (Penguin Books, 1951); Herbert Read, *Contemporary British Art*, rev. edn (Penguin Books, 1964); Malcolm Yorke, *The Spirit of Place* (Constable & Company Ltd, 1988); *Christopher Wood* (Kettle's Yard Gallery, 2013).
71. 'Report on the Session 1953 at Hospitalfield Art College', Hospitalfield Box 1/2, Royal Scottish Academy Archives, Edinburgh.
72. Pages 9–10 of Peggy Beardmore's transcription of: Morris Grassie, interviewed by Peggy Beardmore, 13 March 2014 etc.
73. These developments are discussed in: Edward Gage, *The Eye in the Wind: Contemporary Scottish Painting since 1945* (Collins, 1977); Frederick Gore, *British Painting: 1952–1977* (Royal Academy of Arts, 1977); Herbert Read, *Contemporary British Art*, 1951 & rev. 1964.
74. L.J.A. Bell, 'Scotland's Smallest Art School', *Scotland's Magazine* (1954), p. 26.
75. Bell, 'Scotland's Smallest Art School', p. 29.

4. ARTISTIC INNOVATION, EXPERIMENTATION AND EXCHANGE

1. 'Death of Mr. Patrick Allan Fraser of Hospitalfield', *The Dundee Courier & Argus*, 18 September 1890.
2. See signed guestbooks in the archives of Hospitalfield, Arbroath.
3. 'Do Arbroath Students Receive Benefit from Hospitalfield?', *The Courier*, 15 June 1909, p. 5.
4. For examples see: 'Art Society Proposed for Arbroath', *The Arbroath Herald*, January 1946, p. 25; 'Modern Art', *The Arbroath Herald*, 12 April 1946; 'Hospitalfield Art Students "Discover" Arbroath', *The Arbroath Herald*, 22 October 1948. Evidence can also be found in the archives of the Arbroath Art Society.
5. Paragraph informed by 'Former Art Master', *The Arbroath Herald*, 19 October 1973.
6. The role of Warden was loosely defined by the 1935 Scheme: 'The Warden shall be responsible to the governing body for the management of Hospitalfield House, for the discipline and good order of those resident therein, and for giving such advice and guidance to the students admitted to the Institute as is within his powers.' 'Patrick Allan-Fraser Trust Scheme, 1935: At the Court at Buckingham Palace, the 30th day of April, 1936', p. 11, Box 39, Archives & Collections Centre, Glasgow School of Art, Glasgow.
7. The role of the artist in residence, like that of the Warden, was only loosely defined in the 1935 Scheme: 'With a view to stimulating the student admitted to the benefits of the Institute it shall be in the power of the governing body from time to time to invite distinguished artists to reside as guests at Hospitalfield House'. 'Patrick Allan-Fraser Trust Scheme, 1935: At the Court at Buckingham

Palace, the 30th day of April, 1936', p. 12, Box 39, Archives & Collections Centre, Glasgow School of Art, Glasgow.

8. This type of press was illustrated in E.S. Lumsden's 1925 book *The Art of Etching*, which the students used as an aid to their practice and the press's reassembly.

9. George Donald, conversation with Peggy Beardmore, 24 February 2015.

10. Page 9 of Peggy Beardmore's transcription of Will Maclean, interviewed by Peggy Beardmore, 20 March 2014, EI2014.066, Elphinstone Institute, University of Aberdeen, Aberdeen. This interview also helped inform *Smokies Sold Here* on page 80.

11. George Donald, telephone conversation with Peggy Beardmore, 24 February 2015.

12. Informed through correspondence and conversations with Joyce Cairns, 2016–7.

13. Given the diversity, quantity and visual strength of these images, it is little wonder that when the students exhibited their work in the studios for the Trustees to examine at the end of the summer Cairns was awarded the Hospitalfield Prize.

14. For more on the work of Joyce Cairns see: www.joycecairns.co.uk and Arthur Watson, ed., *War Tourist: An Illustrated Anthology* (Aberdeen City Council, 2006).

15. Jack Knox, 'Report to the Governors of Hospitalfield—1968—by the Guest Artist', Box File 31, Royal Scottish Academy Archives, Edinburgh.

16. Mather and Hamblin shared a room at Hospitalfield and became close friends. This friendship as well as one formed with fellow Hospitalfield student Erick Marwick endured beyond Hospitalfield as Hamblin and Marwick joined Mather in continuing their studies at the Royal College of Art. Mather and Hamblin subsequently shared a flat in London and travelled through Greece together when Mather won a scholarship for landscape painting from the Royal Scottish Academy. Information from email correspondence between Gillian Mather and Peggy Beardmore, 24 February 2014.

17. The prior two paragraphs have been informed by: Jean Martin, interviewed by Peggy Beardmore, 5 November 2014, EI2014.086, Elphinstone Institute, University of Aberdeen, Aberdeen.

18. Adapted from p. 5 of Peggy Beardmore's original transcription of Ian McKenzie Smith, interviewed by Peggy Beardmore, 14 May 2014, EI2014.068, Elphinstone Institute, University of Aberdeen, Aberdeen.

19. 'Minutes of Meeting', 1 December 1955, File 149, *Hospitalfield Patrick Allan Trust: February 1933– March 1961*, Edinburgh College of Art Archives, the University of Edinburgh, Edinburgh.

20. Scotland's connection with Europe, particularly France, is established in Gage, *The Eye in the Wind: Contemporary Scottish Painting since 1945* (Collins, 1977), pp. 11–20.

21. 'Paul Sérusier *The Talisman*', Musée d'Orsay online, 2006, www.musee-orsay.fr/en/collections/ works-in-focus/painting/commentaire_id/the-talisman-7162.html?cHash=fd4aacdb96, accessed 26 July 2016.

22. John Maclauchlan Milne, 'Statement' published on the occasion of the *Exhibition of Contemporary Scottish Painting* at The Gallery, St Andrews, August 1938, reproduced in *John Maclauchlan Milne: 1885–1957* (The Portland Gallery, 2010), p. 96.

23. Adapted from p. 4 of Peggy Beardmore's original transcription from Ian McCulloch, interviewed by Peggy Beardmore, 4 August 2014, EI2014.071, Elphinstone Institute, University of Aberdeen, Aberdeen.

24. Adapted from p. 1 of Peggy Beardmore's original transcription of William Connon, interviewed by Peggy Beardmore, 15 January 2015, EI2015.022, Elphinstone Institute, University of Aberdeen, Aberdeen.

25. Roger Billcliffe, *James McIntosh Patrick* (Fine Arts Society, 1987), pp. 26–7.

26. Page 2 of Peggy Beardmore's transcription of: Ann Patrick, interviewed by Peggy Beardmore, 3 June 2015, EI2015.023, Elphinstone Institute, University of Aberdeen, Aberdeen.

27. James McIntosh Patrick, 'Report on the Students for Session 1957', 8 October 1957, Hospitalfield Box 1/2, *Royal Scottish Academy Letters and Papers*, Royal Scottish Academy Archives, Edinburgh.

28. Richard Hunter interviewed by Cathy Courtney, Tape 19, *NLSC: Artists' Lives*, 2004, British Library, London. *NLSC: Artists' Lives* was an oral history project run by the British Library from 1990 until 2005.

29. James McIntosh Patrick, 'Report on the Students for Session 1957', 8 October 1957, Hospitalfield Box 1/2, *Royal Scottish Academy Letters and Papers*, Royal Scottish Academy Archives, Edinburgh.

30. Adapted from pp. 3, 6 of Peggy Beardmore's original transcription of Ann Patrick, interviewed by Peggy Beardmore, 3 June 2015, EI2015.023, Elphinstone Institute, University of Aberdeen, Aberdeen.

31. Ron Thompson, *Easel in the Field* (Wm Culross & Son Ltd, 2000), p. 3.

32. Thompson, *Easel in the Field*, p. 25.

33. William Buchanan, *Joan Eardley* (Edinburgh University Press, 1976), p. 58; Cordelia Oliver, *Joan Eardley: Memorial Exhibition* (the Scottish Committee of the Arts Council of Great Britain, 1964), p. 18.

34. Page 8 of Peggy Beardmore's transcription of: James Morrison, interviewed by Peggy Beardmore, 30 September 2014, EI2014.085, Elphinstone Institute, University of Aberdeen, Aberdeen. The importance of this belief in Morrison's work and its connection with nineteenth-century French painting is further discussed in John Morrison, *Land and Landscape: The Painting of James Morrison* (The Fleming-Wyfold Art Foundation, 2013), pp. 31–3.

35. The information relating to de Staël was informed by *Nicolas de Staël* (Scottish National Gallery of Modern Art, 1967); Denys Sutton, *Nicolas de Staël* (Evergreen Books, 1960).

36. 'Report on Students by Miss Joan Eardley ARSA', p. 448, *Minute Book Hospitalfield Trust: 1947–1960*, Hospitalfield, Arbroath.

37. 'Report on Students by John Cunningham Esquire', p. 447, *Minute Book Hospitalfield Trust: 1947–1960*, Hospitalfield, Arbroath.

38. Most of Lil Neilson's work from this period is held within private collections. Reproductions of such paintings can be consulted in Ann Steed, *Into the Light: The Art of Lil Neilson* (Aberdeen City Council, 1999).

39. For more about Neilson and her later career see Steed, *Into the Light*.

40. Such parallels are also suggested in Morrison, *Land and Landscape*, pp. 33–4.

41. Similar conclusions to those in the previous two sentences are drawn in Morrison, *Land and Landscape*, p. 38.

42. James Morrison, 'Report on Hospitalfield House Residential Course, 1963', Hospitalfield Box File 31, Royal Scottish Academy Archives, Edinburgh.

43. Page 2 of Peggy Beardmore's transcription of: James Morrison, interviewed by Peggy Beardmore, 30 September 2014, EI2014.085, Elphinstone Institute, University of Aberdeen, Aberdeen.

44. Based on Peggy Beardmore's transcription of Dawson Murray, interviewed by Peggy Beardmore, 5 June 2015, EI2015.035, Elphinstone Institute, University of Aberdeen, Aberdeen.

45. As Roger Billcliffe described regarding the post-war art culture in *The Royal Glasgow Institute of Fine Arts: 1861–1989*, 'few bodies of its size continued to attract the younger generation of experimental painters ... the Institute accepted the situation with complacency.' Roger Billcliffe, Introduction to *The Royal Glasgow Institute of Fine Arts: 1861–1989*, vol. 1 (The Woodend Press, 1990), p. 14.

46. James P. Morrison, 'Modern Art', *The Glasgow Herald*, 30 August 1956.

47. James Spence, Ewan McAslan, Isobel Colville, Anda Paterson, Ian McCulloch, Michael Gill, Rosaleen Orr and Richard Hunter, 'Modern Art in Scotland', *The Glasgow Herald*, 25 August 1956.

48. See 'Letters to the Editor', *The Glasgow Herald*, 24 August–4 September 1956.

49. Page 2 of Peggy Beardmore's transcription of: Ian McCulloch, interviewed by Peggy Beardmore, 4 August 2014, EI2014.071, Elphinstone Institute, University of Aberdeen, Aberdeen.

50. Based on *The Glasgow Group: 1958–2008* (The Glasgow Group, 2008); Margery Palmer McCulloch, 'Young Artists in a "Philistine Society"? Making It New in Glasgow: 1956–1969', *Journal of the Scottish Society for Art History: Art and Art History in Glasgow*, vol. 12 (2007), pp. 69–75; John Morrison, 'The Glasgow Group', *Journal of the Scottish Society for Art History: Art and Art History in Glasgow*, vol. 12 (2007), pp. 62–8.

51. James Bateman, 'A Report on the Work of the Students at the Patrick Allan-Fraser of Hospitalfield Trust School during the Summer Vacation 1955', Hospitalfield Box 1/2, Royal Scottish Academy Archives, Edinburgh.

52. James Cumming, 'Hospitalfield Course, Session July–September, 1962', 26 September 1962, File 149, *Patrick Allan Trust—Hospitalfield Feb. 1960– Oct. 1967*, Edinburgh College of Art Archives, the University of Edinburgh, Edinburgh.

53. James Cumming, 'Hospitalfield Course, Session July–September, 1962', 26 September 1962, File 149, *Patrick Allan Trust—Hospitalfield Feb. 1960– Oct. 1967*, Edinburgh College of Art Archives etc.

54. Page 3 of Peggy Beardmore's transcription of: Alexander Fraser, interviewed by Peggy Beardmore, 17 July 2014, EI2014.070, Elphinstone Institute, University of Aberdeen, Aberdeen.

55. Robert Hewison, *John Byrne: Art and Life* (Lund Humphries, 2011), pp. 23–5.

56. The controversial influence of American Abstract Expressionism in Britain is seen in Gage, *The Eye in the Wind*, p. 22: 'In this period, our lives generally have been dominated by the pressing problem of how to cope with the complications that arise from the astonishing new speed and range of communication. The almost instantaneous dissemination of information has meant that the impact of a brushstroke in New York can swiftly reverberate around the world ... The Scot is a canny man who remains unimpressed by fashionable trends and he prefers to bide his time and question propositions deeply before taking from them what he thinks might be useful.'

57. Frederick Gore, *British Painting: 1952–1977* (Royal Academy of Arts, 1977), p. 10.

58. During the 1950s, Littlejohn was a teacher at Arbroath High School and, due to his previous connections with Hospitalfield, often worked in the studios during the summer.

59. Based on Alan Robb, interviewed by Peggy Beardmore, 10 June 2015, EI2015.35, Elphinstone Institute, University of Aberdeen, Aberdeen.

60. John Miller, 'Report of the Hospitalfield Art College', 1967, Box File 31, Royal Scottish Academy Archives, Edinburgh.

61. Miller, 'Report of the Hospitalfield Art College', 1967, etc.

5. EXPANDING CONNECTIONS AND NEW CHALLENGES

1. Since the Scheme's founding as an Educational Endowment Trust, it had been subject to periodic review by the SED. These reviews resulted in only minor changes being suggested, which the Trustees implemented or ignored at their discretion. When the Scheme's continuance came under question in 1969, the SED and the Trustees took a more active role in governance. While this raised many issues and starting points, none were successfully resolved. For evidence see: letter entitled 'Patrick Allan Fraser Trust' from the Scottish Educational Department, 6 December 1951, File 149, *Hospitalfield Patrick Allan Trust: February 1933–March 1961*, Edinburgh College of Art Archives, the University of Edinburgh, Edinburgh; 'Letter from the Scottish Education Department to the Trustees of Hospitalfield', 19 March 1969, File 149, *Patrick Allan Trust– Hospitalfield October 1967–June 1974*, Edinburgh College of Art Archives, the University of Edinburgh, Edinburgh.

2. 'A new phase in Malcolm's life came with a move up to Arbroath ... During these years Malcolm found the different coastal scenery a fresh source of inspiration ... These pieces were saved to be shown in England on his return there', Monica French, *Evocations* (Art-Amis, 2006), p. 15. During this research, attempts were made to contact Malcolm Fryer to gain greater insight into this period of Hospitalfield's history. Fryer, due to health reasons, declined the offer of interview or correspondence.

3. Malcolm Fryer, 'Appendix A: Report to the Board of Governors of Hospitalfield', November 1971, File 149, *Patrick Allan Trust–Hospitalfield October 1967–June 1974*, Edinburgh College of Art Archives, the University of Edinburgh, Edinburgh.

4. Informed by written recollections by Eugeniusz Jarych, shared with Peggy Beardmore on 13 October 2016.

5. Paragraph informed by: Christoph Greenberg & Laurence Sillars, ed., *Peter Blake* (Tate, 2007), pp. 89–95; Mark Livingstone, *Peter Blake: One Man Show* (Lund Humphries, 2009), pp. 160–7; Nicholas Usherwood, *The Brotherhood of Ruralists* (Lund Humphries, 1981), pp. 6–9.

6. For more see R.V. Weight, *Carel Weight: A Haunted Imagination* (David & Charles, 1993); *Carel Weight, RA* (Royal Academy of Arts, 1982).

7. A discussion of this and reproduction of two of Littlejohn's sketches can be found in Bill Connon, 'Conversations on Cowie', and Joanna Soden, 'The Studio Collection', *William Littlejohn* (The Royal Scottish Academy of Art and Architecture, 2008), pp. 11–3, 18–25.

8. The actual place name of the sandstone cliffs is Dickmont's Den, but it frequently appears as Dickman's Den.

9. Information in this paragraph based on a recorded conversation between Peggy Beardmore and Allan Beveridge on 5 September 2015.

10. 'Appendix D: Some Proposals for the Development of Hospitalfield House', 1969, File 149, *Patrick Allan Trust–Hospitalfield October 1967–June 1974*,

Edinburgh College of Art Archives, the University of Edinburgh, Edinburgh.

11. Page 6 of Peggy Beardmore's transcription of Janet Tod, interviewed by Peggy Beardmore, 2 November 2014, EI2014.083, Elphinstone Institute, University of Aberdeen, Aberdeen.

12. Page 6 of Peggy Beardmore's transcription of Janet Tod, etc. For more about the work of Janet Tod see: www.janettod.co.uk/index.html.

13. Information regarding Kate Whiteford's Hospitalfield experience was informed by a conversation between Peggy Beardmore and Kate Whiteford, 20 June 2014. Also see Mark Irving, 'The Height of Inspiration', *The Evening Standard*, 29 July 1998; 'Whiteford Studio and House', *Kilburn Nightingale Architects* online, www.kilburnnightingale.com/ourwork/articles/articles0306/whitefordstudio.html, accessed 26 July 2016.

14. Adapted from p. 7 of Peggy Beardmore's original transcription of Lennox Dunbar, interviewed by Peggy Beardmore, 2 December 2014, EI2014.087, Elphinstone Institute, University of Aberdeen, Aberdeen.

15. Several attempts were made throughout this research process to contact William Payne. A reply was never received. This section therefore relies on archival sources and the oral history of former Hospitalfield students and artists in residence to assess the events of this period and their significance in Hospitalfield's history. In addition, a reliable birth date could not be confirmed from available sources.

16. This issue was first raised at a 1968 sub-committee meeting of the Trustees. 'The Sub-committee of Principals', 17 October 1968, File 149, *Patrick Allan Trust–Hospitalfield October 1967–June 1974*, Edinburgh College of Art Archives, the University of Edinburgh, Edinburgh.

17. William Payne, 'Annual Report to the Trustees Concerning Activities at Hospitalfield in 1992', 1992, Box File 32, Royal Scottish Academy Archives, Edinburgh.

18. This trend is discussed in *The Vigorous Imagination: New Scottish Art* (The Trustees of the National Galleries of Scotland, 1987).

19. Robert Heller, *Peter Howson* (Mainstream Publishing, 1993), p. 15.

20. Derived from correspondence between Gwen Hardie and Peggy Beardmore, 6 May 2014. For more about the artist see: www.gwenhardie.com.

21. Pages 4 and 5 of Peggy Beardmore's transcription of: Susan Forsyth, interviewed by Peggy Beardmore, 6 November 2014, EI2014.088, Elphinstone Institute, University of Aberdeen, Aberdeen.

22. Quotation from a recorded conversation between Claire Ashley and Peggy Beardmore, 2 January 2014.

23. Adapted from p. 5 of Peggy Beardmore's original transcription of Alexander Fraser, interviewed by Peggy Beardmore, 17 July 2014, EI2014.070, Elphinstone Institute, University of Aberdeen, Aberdeen.

24. Transcribed from a recorded conversation between Joe McIntyre and Peggy Beardmore, 5 September 2015.

25. Adapted from p. 4 of Peggy Beardmore's original transcription of Frances Walker, interviewed by

Peggy Beardmore, 24 April 2014, EI2014.067, Elphinstone Institute, University of Aberdeen, Aberdeen.

26. For more about Ashley's practice see Claire Ashley, *Artist Statement*, 2016, http://claireashley.com/statement.html, accessed 26 July 2016.

27. Derrick Guild attended Hospitalfield in 1985 from DJCA; for more see: http://derrickguild.com, accessed 26 July 2016. Angus McEwan attended Hospitalfield in 1986 from DJCA; for more see: www.angusmcewan.com, accessed 26 July 2016. Joseph Urie attended Hospitalfield in 1980 from DJCA; for more see: www.fidrafineart.co.uk/index.php/artists/view/urie-joseph, accessed 26 July 2016. Andrew Stenhouse attended Hospitalfield in 1977 from DJCA; for more see: www.royalscottishacademy.org/members/andrew-stenhouse, accessed 26 July 2016. Callum Innes attended Hospitalfield from Gray's School of Art in 1983; for more see: www.calluminnes.com, accessed 26 July 2016.

28. Susan Kraut, 'Susan Kraut', *Addington Gallery* online, http://danaddington.com/addingtongallery/kraut/kraut.html, accessed 14 July 2017.

29. For evidence of the impact of the Environmental Art Department upon the development of twenty-first-century Scottish art see Moira Jeffrey, ed., *Generation Guide & Reader* (Trustees of the National Galleries of Scotland and Glasgow Life, 2014).

30. 'The Patrick Allan-Fraser Trust Scheme 1980', 1980, Box File 32, Royal Scottish Academy Archives, Edinburgh.

31. Information from a recorded conversation between Alan Robb and Peggy Beardmore, 10 June 2015.

32. Wendy McMurdo attended Hospitalfield from ECA in 1983; for more see: http://wendymcmurdo.com, accessed 26 July 2016. Donald Urquhart attended Hospitalfield from GSA in 1981; for more see: www.educationscotland.gov.uk/marksonthelandscape/artistsandnature/artists/donaldurquhart/index.asp, accessed 26 July 2016, and www.saatchigallery.com/artists/donald_urquhart.htm, accessed 26 July 2016. Kristin Mojsiewicz attended Hospitalfield as a sculpture student from ECA in 1993; for more see: www.eca.ed.ac.uk/school-of-art/kristin-mojsiewicz, accessed 26 July 2016. Jane Benson attended Hospitalfield from ECA in 1993; for more see: http://janebenson.net, accessed 26 July 2016. Cordelia Underwood attended Hospitalfield in 1993 from DJCA; for more see: www.dundee.ac.uk/djcad/exhibitions/exhibitions/entrance-offsite, accessed 26 July 2016.

33. Adapted from pp. 7–8 of Peggy Beardmore's original transcription of Mae McKenzie Smith, interviewed by Peggy Beardmore, 14 May 2014, EI2014.069, Elphinstone Institute, University of Aberdeen, Aberdeen.

34. Based on a recorded conversation between Alistair MacLennan and Peggy Beardmore, 21 November 2015.

CONCLUSION

1. Charles Robert Swift, *Hospitalfield: The Home of the Antiquary* (St Albans, 1952), pp. 18, 20.

Select bibliography

PRIMARY SOURCES

Archives

'Hospitalfield Patrick Allan Trust', File 149, Edinburgh College of Art Archives, University of Edinburgh, Edinburgh.

'Minute Books of the Hospitalfield Trust' in six volumes divided by years: 1890–95, 1895–1907, 1907–21, 1921–36, 1936–46, Hospitalfield, Arbroath.

'Papers of Sir Harry J. Barnes, Director of Glasgow School of Art, 1964–80', Boxes 13, 23, 26, 36 and 39, the Glasgow School of Art Archives and Collections, Glasgow (Archive Reference: GSAA/DIR/13).

'RSA Letters & Papers', Archive Box, Hospitalfield 1/2, Hospitalfield 2/2, Box Files 31, 32, 164, Royal Scottish Academy of Art and Architecture Archives, Edinburgh.

Oral history interviews

Connon, William, interviewed by Peggy Beardmore, 15 January 2015, EI2015.022,

Dunbar, Lennox, interviewed by Peggy Beardmore, 2 December 2014, EI2014.087.

Elphinstone Institute, University of Aberdeen, Aberdeen. *All subsequent interviews in this list are housed at the University of Aberdeen's Elphinstone Institute.*

Forsyth, Susan, interviewed by Peggy Beardmore, 6 November 2014, EI2014.088.

Fraser, Alexander, interviewed by Peggy Beardmore, 17 July 2014, EI2014.070.

Grassie, Morris, interviewed by Peggy Beardmore, 13 March 2014, EI2014.064.

Lockhart, David, interviewed by Peggy Beardmore, 28 October 2014, EI2014.084.

Maclean, Will, interviewed by Peggy Beardmore, 20 March 2014, EI2014.066.

Martin, Jean, interviewed by Peggy Beardmore, 5 November 2014, EI2014.086.

McCulloch, Ian, interviewed by Peggy Beardmore, 4 August 2014, EI2014.071.

Morrison, James, interviewed by Peggy Beardmore, 30 September 2014, EI2014.085.

Murray, Dawson, interviewed by Peggy Beardmore, 6 June 2015, EI2015.034.

Patrick, Ann, interviewed by Peggy Beardmore, 3 June 2015, EI2015.023.

Robb, Alan, interviewed by Peggy Beardmore, 10 June 2015, EI2015.035.

Robertson, Hugh, interviewed by Peggy Beardmore, 18 March 2014, EI2014.065.

Smith, Ian McKenzie, interviewed by Peggy Beardmore, 14 May 2014, EI2014.068.

Smith, Mae McKenzie, interviewed by Peggy Beardmore, 14 May 2014, EI2014.069.

Tod, Janet, interviewed by Peggy Beardmore, 2 November 2014, EI2014.083.

Walker, Frances, interviewed by Peggy Beardmore, 24 April 2014, EI2014.067.

SECONDARY SOURCES

Andreae, Christopher. *Joan Eardley.* Farnham: Lund Humphries, 2013.

Andrew, Patricia R. *A Chasm in Time.* Edinburgh: Birlinn, 2014.

Baldry, Alfred Lys. *Hubert von Herkomer, RA: A Study and a Biography.* London: George Bell and Sons, 1901.

Bell, L.J.A. 'Scotland's Smallest Art School'. *Scotland's Magazine,* September (1954): 24–9.

Billcliffe, Roger. *Ian Fleming, RSA, RSW, RGI.* Edinburgh: The Fine Art Society, 1991.

Billcliffe, Roger. *James McIntosh Patrick.* London: The Fine Arts Society, 1987.

Billcliffe, Roger. *The Royal Glasgow Institute of Fine Arts: 1861–1989.* Glasgow: The Woodend Press, 1990.

Bliss, Douglas Percy. *James Cowie: 1886–1956.* Edinburgh: The Arts Council Scottish Committee, 1957.

Bowness, Sophie, ed. *Carving Mountains: Modern Stone Sculpture in England: 1907–1937.* Cambridge: Kettle's Yard, 1998.

Bristow, Roger. *The Last Bohemians.* Bristol: Sansom & Company, 2010.

Brown, Alison. *Ian Fleming: A Major Retrospective Exhibition.* Aberdeen: Aberdeen Art Gallery and Museum, 1996.

Bruce, George. *William Burns.* Aberdeen: Aberdeen Art Gallery, 1973.

Buchanan, William. *Joan Eardley.* Edinburgh: Edinburgh University Press, 1976.

Calvocoressi, Richard. *James Cowie.* Edinburgh: Scottish National Gallery of Modern Art, 1979.

Campbell, Mungo. *The Line of Tradition: Watercolours, Drawings and Prints by Scottish Artists: 1700–1990.* Edinburgh: The Trustees of the National Galleries of Scotland, 1993.

Caw, James L. *Scottish Painting Past and Present: 1620–1908.* Bath: Kingsmead Reprints, 1975.

Co, Griffin, ed. *Frances Walker.* Aberdeen: Aberdeen City Council, 2009.

Connon, Bill. 'James Cowie, Painter'. *Leopard Magazine,* July/August (2002): 43–4.

Devaney, Maria. *Mountain, Meadow, Moss and Moor.* Stirling: Stirling Smith Art Gallery and Museum, 1996.

Edwards, Lee MacCormick. *Herkomer: A Victorian Artist.* Aldershot: Ashgate Publishing, 1999.

Errington, Lindsay. *Master Class: Robert Scott Lauder and His Pupils.* Edinburgh: The Trustees of the National Galleries of Scotland, 1983.

Fiddes, Jim, and Ross Hayworth, eds. *Gray's 120.* Aberdeen: The Robert Gordon University, 2005.

Finlay, Ian. *The Story of Scots Architecture.* Edinburgh: Douglas & Foulis, 1951.

Fraser, Patrick Allan. *An Unpopular View of Our Times.* Edinburgh: Myles Macphail, 1861.

French, Monica. *Evocations.* Hitchin: Art-Amis, 2006.

Gage, Edward. *The Eye in the Wind: Contemporary Scottish Painting since 1945.* London: Collins, 1977.

Gibson, Colin. 'The Art of James Cowie'. *The Scots Magazine,* vol. LV, no. 3 (1951): 177–84.

Gifford, John. *The Buildings of Scotland: Dundee and Angus.* London: Yale University Press, 2012.

Gordon, Esme. *The Royal Scottish Academy of Painting, Sculpture & Architecture: 1826–1976.* Edinburgh: Charles Skilton Ltd, 1976.

Gore, Frederick. *British Painting: 1952–1977.* London: The Royal Academy of Arts, 1977.

Halsby, Julian. *Scottish Watercolours: 1740–1940.* London: B.T. Batsford, 1986.

Hardie, William. *Scottish Painting: 1837–Present,* 3rd ed. Glasgow: Waverley Books, 2010.

Hare, Bill. *Contemporary Painting in Scotland.* Tortola: Craftsman House, 1992.

Hartley, Keith. *Scottish Art since 1900.* London: Lund Humphries, 1989.

Hay, George, ed. *The Book of Hospitalfield: A Memorial of Patrick Allan-Fraser HRSA of Hospitalfield.* Privately Printed for the Hospitalfield Trustees, 1894.

Helland, Janice. *Professional Women Painters in Nineteenth-century Scotland.* Aldershot: Ashgate Publishing, 2000.

Heller, Robert. *Peter Howson.* Edinburgh: Mainstream Publishing, 1993.

Hewison, Robert. *John Byrne: Art and Life.* Farnham: Lund Humphries, 2011.

James, Merlin and David Stephenson. *Ray Howard-Jones: The Elements of Art.* Blewbury: The Rocket Press, 1993.

Jarron, Matthew. *Independent and Individualist.* Dundee: Abertay Historical Society, 2015.

Jason, Neville, and Lisa Thompson-Pharoah. *The Sculpture of Frank Dobson.* Herts: The Henry Moore Foundation, 1994.

Jeffrey, Moira, ed. *Generation: 25 Years of Contemporary Art in Scotland: Reader and Guide.* Trustees of the National Galleries of Scotland and Glasgow Life, 2014.

Lees, G. Frederic. 'The Art of George Harcourt'. *The Studio,* vol. LXX (1917): 160–9.

Livingstone, Marco. *Peter Blake.* Farnham: Lund Humphries, 2009.

Longman, Grant. *The Herkomer Art School and Subsequent Development: 1901–1918.* Bushey: E.G. Longman, 1981.

Lübbren, Nina. *Rural Artists' Colonies in Europe: 1870–1910.* Manchester: Manchester University Press, 2001.

Macdonald, Murdo. *Scottish Art.* London: Thames & Hudson, 2000.

Macmillan, Duncan. *Scottish Art: 1460–2000,* 2nd ed. Edinburgh: Mainstream Publishing, 2000.

Matthews, Joan M. *J.B. Souter: 1890–1971.* Perth: Perth Museum and Art Gallery, 1990.

McClure, David. 'R. Henderson Blyth (1919–1970)'. *Scottish Art Review,* vol. XII, no. 3 (1972): 21–2, 31.

McCulloch, Felix. *Four Scottish Artists.* Edinburgh: The Scottish Committee of the Arts Council of Great Britain, 1964.

McCulloch, Margery Palmer. 'Young Artists in a "Philistine Society"? Making It New in Glasgow: 1956–1969'. *Journal of the Scottish Society for Art History: Art and Art History in Glasgow,* vol. 12 (2007): 69–75.

McKenzie, Ray, ed. *The Flower and the Green Leaf.* Edinburgh: Luath Press Ltd, 2009.

Millar, A.H. 'Hospitalfield: A Proposed College for Artists'. *Art Journal* (1896): 246–8.

Morrison, John. 'The Glasgow Group'. *Journal of the*

Scottish Society for Art History: Art and Art History in Glasgow, vol. 12 (2007): 62–8.

Morrison, John. *Land and Landscape: The Painting of James Morrison*. London: The Fleming-Wyfold Art Foundation, 2013.

Morrison, John. *Painting Labour in Scotland and Europe: 1805–1910*. Aldershot: Ashgate Publishing, 2014.

Morrison, John. *Particles of Light*. Aberdeen: Robert Gordon University, 2000.

Oliver, Cordelia. *Angus Neil*. Aberdeen: Arts and Recreation Division, City of Aberdeen District Council, 1994.

Oliver, Cordelia. *Jack Knox: Paintings and Drawings 1960–1983*. Glasgow: Third Eye Centre, 1983.

Oliver, Cordelia. *James Cowie*. Edinburgh: Edinburgh University Press, 1980.

Oliver, Cordelia. *James Cowie: The Artist at Work*. Edinburgh: Scottish Arts Council, 1981.

Oliver, Cordelia. *Joan Eardley: Memorial Exhibition*. Edinburgh: The Scottish Committee of the Arts Council of Great Britain, 1964.

Oliver, Cordelia. *Joan Eardley, RSA*. Edinburgh: Mainstream Publishing, 1988.

Oliver, Cordelia. *Ten Artists from North East Scotland*. Aberdeen: Aberdeen Art Gallery and Museum and Bergen Kunst-Forening, 1979.

Paterson, James. 'A Note on Nationality in Art'. *The Scottish Art Review*, vol. 1, no. 3 (1888): 89–90.

Payne, William. *Hospitalfield*. Edinburgh: The Trustees of the National Galleries of Scotland, 1990.

Pearson, Fiona. *Joan Eardley*. Edinburgh: National Galleries of Scotland, 2007.

Pope, Carol, ed. *Hospitalfield House*. Arbroath: Patrick Allan-Fraser of Hospitalfield Trust, 2011.

Rennie, Paul. *Modern British Posters*. London: Black Dog Publishing, 2010.

Rhynd, James. 'Hospitalfield'. *The Scots Magazine*, November (1947): 93–100.

Richardson, Craig. *Scottish Art since 1960*. Burlington: Ashgate Publishing, 2010.

Setford, David. *Stand by Your Work: Hubert von Herkomer and His Students*. Watford: Borough Council, 1983

Smith, Bill, and Selina Skipwith. *A History of Scottish Art*. London: Merrell Publishers, 2003.

Spielman, M.H. 'To Whom It May Concern: The New Free Art University'. *The Magazine of Art* (1901): 507–11.

Steed, Ann. *Into the Light: The Art of Lil Neilson*. Aberdeen: Aberdeen City Council, 1999.

Strang, Alice. *Consider the Lilies: Scottish Painting 1910–1980*. Dundee: Dundee City Council, 2006.

Strang, Alice, ed. *Modern Scottish Women: Painters and Sculptors 1885–1965*. Edinburgh: Trustees of the National Galleries of Scotland, 2015.

Swift, Charles Robert. *Hospitalfield: The Home of the Antiquary*. St Albans: Charles Robert Swift, 1952.

Thompson, Ron. *Easel in the Field*. Coupar: Wm Culross & Son Ltd, 2000.

Weight, R.V. *Carel Weight: A Haunted Imagination*. Devon: David & Charles, 1993.

Whyte, Anne, ed. *Ian Fleming: Graphic Work*. Aberdeen: Peacock Printmakers, 1983.

Wishart, Anne, ed. *The Society of Scottish Artists: The First 100 Years*. Edinburgh: The Society of Scottish Artists, 1991.

Hospitalfield participants

THE GOVERNORS AND STUDENTS OF THE ALLAN-FRASER ART COLLEGE 1901–28

Governor 1901–9: George Harcourt

Students admitted 1902: Evelyn Brewer; Frederick B. Hassall; William D. Hopkins; Arthur F. Jenkins; William Maclean; Arthur M. Pinion; Charles Robert Swift; Charles S. Williams.
Students admitted 1903: Robert Clarence Abercromby; James Anderson; Thomas Percival Anderson; Horace J. Castle; William E. Daly; David P. Davidson; Oliver Garbet; Ewan W. Gold; Theobald B. Gould; William B. Huntly; Ernest Johnson; Arnold H. Mason; John W. Palmer; Allan Newton Sutherland; John Thomson; John Trail.
Students admitted 1906: Bernard R. Adams; Austin C. Cooper; Frank Dobson; Brian Hatton; John Arthur Machray Hay; Cecil S. Jamieson; John 'Jack' M.S. Orr; Adam Sheriff Scott; Robert Timmis; Richard C. West.

Governor 1909–26: Peter Munnoch

Student admitted 1909: John Bulloch Souter.
Students admitted 1910: Arthur Copeland; Arthur Crossland; Kenneth Forbes; Adam George Galloway; Stanley Horace Gardiner; David Nicholson Inglis; David Morris; David Wood Murray; Horace Grimshaw Payne Ovenden.
Student admitted 1912: Alan Fawns Anderson.
Students admitted 1913: Harold Hookway Cowles; John Davidson; James Alexander Garden; William John Macleod; George Cunningham Stevenson; Percy Telford; John Thomas Alexander Waddell; Hubert Thomas Ward; Albert John Warr.
Students admitted 1915: Arnold Corbluth; Francis Gerald Firth.
Students admitted 1916: William E. Ireland; Alexander C. Lyall; Archie McVicar.
Students admitted 1917: Thomas McGregor Douglas; Cuthbert Bernard Lupton; Francis Thomas Henry Oldham.
Student admitted 1919: Arthur Hincliffe.
Students admitted 1920: Arthur Charles Boodle; Arthur Gaffron; James Albert Lambert; Robert Leonard White.
Student admitted 1923: Edward Kitchener Center.
Students admitted 1925: Thomas Burden; Alexander Charles Koolman; Norman E. Manners; Joseph Webb.

Governor 1926–8: Henry Daniel

Student admitted 1926: Charles Christie Ruxton.
Students admitted 1927: Edward Wilson Murray Marr; William George Scoular.

PARTICIPANTS OF THE PATRICK ALLAN-FRASER TRUST SCHEME 1937–94

*Female artists have been listed with the surnames they were known by at the time of their participation.

Warden 1937–48: James Cowie

Students 1937
Dundee College of Art: George Wright.

Edinburgh College of Art: Carnegie Brown; David Mathers; Alexander McDonald.
Glasgow School of Art: John Whyte.
Gray's School of Art: Meeda Inglis.
Students 1938
Edinburgh College of Art: Neil Russell.
Glasgow School of Art: Robert Henderson Blyth; Robert Colquhoun; John Laurie; Robert MacBryde; John Miller.
Ayr Academy: Waistel Cooper.
Students 1939
Dundee College of Art: Alexander Allan; Patrick Hennessy; Harry Keay.
Edinburgh College of Art: Charles Pulsford; Robert Thompson.
Ayr Academy: Waistel Cooper.
Harris Art School, Preston: Joseph Heaton.
Nottingham Art School: Leslie Marshall.
Students 1940
Edinburgh College of Art: Alexander Robertson.
Glasgow School of Art: Ralph Draper; John Laurie; John Miller; Frances E. Stewart.
Gray's School of Art: Hamish Laurie; Francesca Ludwig; George Scott.
Cardiff College of Art: Adeline Barnett.
Hornley School of Art, London: Angela Francis.
Todmorden School, Yorkshire: Ernest Calvert.
Students 1941
Dundee College of Art: Winifred Allan; John McCormack.
Glasgow School of Art: Isabel Brodie Babianska; Marie de Banzie; Bertha West.
School of Art at King's College, Newcastle: Olive M. Hicks.
privately trained: Brian Harding.
Royal College of Art: Margery Hall.
Students 1942
Dundee College of Art: Winifred Allan; Joan Cuthill.
Glasgow School of Art: Frederick Day; Christina Mackay; Agnes Saxon; Elizabeth Thompson.
Arbroath High School: Euphemia Findlay; George Grassie.
Mansfield School of Art: Emmeline Thompson.
Students 1943
Edinburgh College of Art: Heather Corlass; Westby Prescott.
Glasgow School of Art: Mildred Hobden; Mary McAllister; Inga Svargo; Donald Swan.
Arbroath High School: George Grassie.
Students 1944
Edinburgh College of Art: David Lockhart; William McLaren.
Glasgow School of Art: John Cunningham; Patricia O'Donnell; Cordelia Patrick
Convent of Our Lady of Chepstow, London: Patricia Ambrose.
Students 1945
Dundee College of Art: Alison Clark; Euphemia Findlay.
Edinburgh College of Art: Agnes Johnston.
Glasgow School of Art: Joan Doherty; Elizabeth 'Bet' Low.
Students 1946
Dundee College of Art: William Littlejohn; Sadie Stephen; George Wright.
Edinburgh College of Art: Donald Rudd.
Glasgow School of Art: Robert Henderson Blyth; Alexander Young.
Hammersmith Art School, London: Myona Fisher.

Leeds College of Art: Joyce Metcalf.
Slade School of Fine Art: Rosemary Howard-Jones.
Students 1947
Glasgow School of Art: Nita Begg; Joan Eardley; William Gallacher.
Arbroath – no formal training: Angus Neil.
Liverpool College of Art: Margaret Walker.

Warden 1948–54: Ian Fleming

Students 1948
Edinburgh College of Art: Ester Hamilton.
Glasgow School of Art: William Burns; James Goodwin; Avril Lunn; Roy McComish; Iain McKenzie; William Mitchell; Robert Robertson; Robert Simpson.
Gray's School of Art: Edith Bishop.
Students 1949
Dundee College of Art: Andrew Neilson.
Edinburgh College of Art: William Clyne; Erik Forrest; Alexander Hoskins.
Glasgow School of Art: William Burns; Thomas Gordon Moffat; Hugh Robertson.
Hammersmith School of Art, London: Lawrence Eveleigh.
Students 1950
Dundee College of Art: Oscar Goodall.
Edinburgh College of Art: Douglas Baxter; Zigmunt Bukowoki; Alistair Flattley; James Hardie.
Glasgow School of Art: Cameron Bannerman; Richard Binnie; William Birnie.
Students 1951
Dundee College of Art: John Nicol.
Edinburgh College of Art: Daniel Clyne; Helmut Petzsch; James Syme.
Glasgow School of Art: Richard Binnie; William Birnie; Lawrence Gordon; Drummond Mayo; William Russell.
Visiting artist 1952: Joan Eardley.
Students 1952
Dundee College of Art: Morris Grassie.
Edinburgh College of Art: Ella Leslie; Thelma McDonald; Frances Walker.
Glasgow School of Art: Archibald Graham; Gavin Nicol; Forbes Yule.
Visiting artist 1953: William Burns.
Students 1953
Dundee College of Art: John Clark; Morris Grassie; Douglas Swan.
Glasgow School of Art: Nan Bryden; Elizabeth McKenzie; Gordon Wyllie.
Arbroath High School: Margaret Baxter.
Goldsmiths, London: Michael Canney.

Warden 1954–70: William Reid

Students 1954
Edinburgh College of Art: David Ewans; Herbert Jones; William Millar; Myra Soni.
Glasgow School of Art: Katherine Forrest; Jennifer Ritchie.
Artist in residence 1955: James Bateman.
Students 1955
Dundee College of Art: William Cadenhead; Kenneth C.B. Patterson.
Glasgow School of Art: Elizabeth McMaster; James Robertson; Margaret Roger.
Gray's School of Art: William Crocket; Moira Maitland.

Artist in residence 1956: John Maclauchlan Milne.
Students 1956
  Dundee College of Art: Richard Hunter.
  Glasgow School of Art: Isobel Colville;
  Ewan McAslan; Ian McCulloch; Rosaleen Orr;
  Anda Paterson; James Spence.
  Gray's School of Art: Michael Gill.
Artist in residence 1957–9: James McIntosh Patrick.
Students 1957
  Dundee College of Art: Allan Buick; Ann Patrick.
  Glasgow School of Art: Jack Knox; Anda Paterson;
  Jean Stevenson.
  Gray's School of Art: William Connon;
  Ian McKenzie Smith.
Students 1958
  Dundee College of Art: Neil Dallas Brown;
  Patricia Gordon.
  Glasgow School of Art: Diana de Fenzi; Jean Fleming;
  Mae Fotheringham.
  Gray's School of Art: Ian McKenzie Smith;
  Ann McWilliam.
Students 1959
  Dundee College of Art: Dennis Buchan;
  Ian Drummond; Elizabeth Hill.
  Edinburgh College of Art: Jean Beattie.
  Glasgow School of Art: Diana Christie;
  David Paterson; Duncan Shanks.
  Gray's School of Art: Ian Massie.
Artists in residence 1960: John Cunningham;
  Joan Eardley
Students 1960
  Dundee College of Art: George Brown; Lilian Neilson;
  Sheelagh Wrigglesworth.
  Glasgow School of Art: Pat Boyle; Diana Christie;
  Thomas Craig.
  Gray's School of Art: Evelyn Farquharson;
  Kenneth Ormonde.
Artist in residence 1961–2: James Cumming.
Students 1961
  Dundee College of Art:David Strachan.
  Glasgow School of Art: John Byrne; Maureen Lusk;
  Hugh McGinley; Betty Patterson.
  Gray's School of Art: Don Boyd; Alexander Fraser.
Students 1962
  Edinburgh College of Art: Ethel Hope;
  Geoffrey Roper.
  Glasgow School of Art: Kathryn Kynoch;
  Peter MacCallum.
  Gray's School of Art: Michael Benzie;
  Michael Farningham; Alish Farrell.
Artist in residence 1963–4: James Morrison.
Students 1963
  Duncan of Jordanstone College of Art and Design:
  James Boyd; Emilio Joachim.
  Edinburgh College of Art: Chloe Brayne;
  Robert Hubbard.
  Glasgow School of Art: Rosemary Atkins;
  Kathryn Kynoch; Patricia Munro.
  Gray's School of Art: John Crawford; Ian Nicoll.
Students 1964
  Duncan of Jordanstone: Joe McIntyre;
  Malcolm Nicoll; Gwen Swan; Elizabeth Watson.
  Glasgow School of Art: Hugh Fletcher; Patricia
  Munro; Dawson Murray; Lindsay Nelson.
  Gray's School of Art: Brownlie Armour;
  William Inglis.
Artist in residence 1965–6: David McClure.
Students 1965
  Duncan of Jordanstone: Robert Crerar; Jean Knox;
  Alistair MacLennan.
  Edinburgh College of Art: George Donald;
  Frances Sanders.
  Glasgow School of Art: Alexander Houston;
  Neil Morrison; Richard Robertson.
  Gray's School of Art: Will Maclean;
  John Stenhouse.

Students 1966
  Duncan of Jordanstone: Margaret Cuthbert;
  Jennifer Lamont.
  Edinburgh College of Art: Alistair Wright;
  Alan J. Wright.
  Glasgow School of Art: Bruce Gould;
  Jennifer Kinghorn; Deidre McCartin.
  Gray's School of Art: David Alistair Crighton;
  Alan Morrice; Rosemary Richardson.
Artist in residence 1967: John Miller.
Students 1967
  Duncan of Jordanstone: Eric Marwick;
  Raymond McGowan; Calum McKenzie.
  Edinburgh College of Art: William Brereton;
  Rosemary Hamblin; Gillian Mather.
  Glasgow School of Art: Jean Campbell;
  David Croft-Smith; Valerie Houston.
  Gray's School of Art: Ian Coutts; Martin Davidson;
  Ian Guthrie.
Artist in residence 1968–9: Jack Knox.
Students 1968
  Duncan of Jordanstone: Douglas Gray;
  Christopher Moore; Cameron Thomson.
  Edinburgh College of Art: Christopher J. Allan;
  Elaine Lawrence; Anna Small.
  Glasgow School of Art: Robin Hume; Taeusz Klasicki;
  Elice Rae.
  Gray's School of Art: Gillies Campbell;
  Anne Patterson; Alan Robb; Christine Rutherford.
Students 1969
  Duncan of Jordanstone: Michael Cox;
  Andrea E.J. Duncan; Alexander Stobie.
  Edinburgh College of Art: James McGlade;
  Glen Onwin; Ian G. Robertson.
  Glasgow School of Art: Barry H. Blair;
  Donald K. Manson; James McNaught.
  Gray's School of Art: Joyce Cairns; Hugh T. Rowson;
  Robert H. Stevens.

Warden 1970–6: Malcolm Fryer

Artist in residence 1970: Cyril Reason.
Students 1970
  Duncan of Jordanstone: Joyce Fisher;
  Marjorie Hamilton; John Wallace.
  Edinburgh College of Art: Alan Archibald;
  John Mooney; Katherine Pow.
  Glasgow School of Art: George Birrell; James Wales;
  Eric Young.
  Gray's School of Art: Robert E. Donald;
  Stuart W. MacDonald; Isobel S. Smith.
Artist in residence 1971: Robert Callender.
Students 1971
  Duncan of Jordanstone: Clark Nicol;
  Joseph Smernicki; Janet Tod.
  Edinburgh College of Art: John Millard;
  Richard White; Sandy Young.
  Glasgow School of Art: Sadie Bookless;
  Yvonne Brodie; Craig McKenchnie.
  Gray's School of Art: Allan Lawson; Ann Murray;
  David Pettigrew.
Artists in residence 1972: Richard Hunter;
  William Littlejohn.
Students 1972
  Duncan of Jordanstone: John Mallinder;
  Alexandra McNeillance; Ann Spinks.
  Edinburgh College of Art: John Bissett; Brent Millar;
  Nicola Weal.
  Glasgow School of Art: Alexander Graham;
  Glen Scouller; Kate Whiteford.
  Gray's School of Art: Kenneth Donaldson;
  Maurice Jackson; Ian Oates.
Artist in residence 1973, 1975, 1976: Peter Blake.
Students 1973
  Duncan of Jordanstone: Patricia McCabe;
  Jack Morrocco; Albert Sinclair.

Edinburgh College of Art: Judith Heller;
  Kate Maclean; Gavin Robson.
  Glasgow School of Art: Sylvia Black; David Blair;
  Linda Turner.
  Gray's School of Art: Roy Benzies; Lennox Dunbar;
  John Inglis
Artist in residence 1974: Carel Weight.
Students 1974
  Duncan of Jordanstone: Eugeniusz Jarych;
  Eddie Marra; Brian Norman.
  Edinburgh College of Art: Charlotte Bryce;
  Gerry Callaghan; Christine Ironside.
  Glasgow School of Art: Paddy Dorrian; Helen Wilson.
  Gray's School of Art: Betty Blease; Hugh Gilmour;
  Sandy Reid.
Students 1975
  Duncan of Jordanstone: Robin Dickson; Peter Horobin.
  Edinburgh College of Art: Janis Dougall; Gus Maclean;
  Andrew Neil; Susan Smith; Ruth Stiven.
  Glasgow School of Art: Gail Harvey; Gordon Mackie;
  Tony McConologue.
  Gray's School of Art: Catriona Beaton;
  Ewan McArthur; Gordon McDowall.
Students 1976
  Duncan of Jordanstone: Allan Beveridge;
  Alexander Gillian; Donald Sutherland.
  Edinburgh College of Art: Judith Lasson;
  Catherine Mayo.
  Glasgow School of Art: Tony McConologue;
  Donald Sutherland; Brian Ward.
  Gray's School of Art: John Ross; Alistair Tatton.

Warden, Autumn 1976–94: William Payne

Artist in residence 1977: Alexander Fraser.
Students 1977
  Duncan of Jordanstone: Robert Montgomery;
  Philip Pilkington; Andrew Stenhouse.
  Edinburgh College of Art: Robert McNeill;
  Michael Singleton; Fiona Strickland; Paula Wheal.
  Glasgow School of Art: Linda Anton; David Ellie;
  Douglas Thomson.
  Gray's School of Art: Keith Byres; Helen Fergus;
  David Henderson.
Artist in residence 1978: Iain Patterson
Students 1978
  Duncan of Jordanstone: Louise Cattrell;
  Susie Patterson; Fiona Redler.
  Edinburgh College of Art: Judith Glennie;
  Thora Hamilton; Stella Sanderman.
  Glasgow School of Art: Maureen Binnie;
  Neil Macdonald; John McLaughlin.
  Gray's School of Art: Elizabeth Cussiter;
  Ian Robertson; Morna Whyte
Artists in residence 1979: Peter Collins;
  Alexander Fraser; Joseph McIntyre.
Students 1979
  Duncan of Jordanstone: Catriona Herd; Fiona Phillips.
  Edinburgh College of Art: Caroline Byres;
  Robin Payne; Catriona White.
  Glasgow School of Art: Crawford Campbell;
  David Fallen; Leslie Main; Sandy Murphy.
  Gray's School of Art: Ian Brady; Dawn Burgess;
  Helen Pomphrey; Morna Whyte.
Artists in residence 1980: John Grant Clifford;
  Peter Collins.
Students 1980
  Duncan of Jordanstone: Michael McVeigh; Peter Seal;
  Joseph Urie.
  Edinburgh College of Art: Alistair Hearslim;
  Kirsty Kirkwood; Alistair Strachan.
  Glasgow School of Art: John Docherty; Peter Howson;
  Moira Scott.
  Gray's School of Art: Christine Drummond;
  Gareth Edwards; Douglas Webster.
Artist in residence 1981: Richard C. Blomfield.

Students 1981
  Duncan of Jordanstone: Keith McIntyre; Leslie Milne;
  Sheenagh Patience.
  Edinburgh College of Art: Claire Devine;
  Lesley Findlayson; Christina McGown.
  Glasgow School of Art: Terry Quinn; Ruth Stirling;
  Donald Urquart.
  Gray's School of Art: George Cheyne; Keith Grant;
  Graham Johnstone.
Artist in residence 1982: Douglas Kemp.
Students 1982
  Duncan of Jordanstone: David Cook; Michael Windle;
  Susan Winton.
  Edinburgh College of Art: Gwen Hardie;
  Stuart McKenzie; Robert McLaurin.
  Glasgow School of Art: Ann Campbell;
  Catriona McDonald; Christine Peters.
  Gray's School of Art: Graham Curran; Alistair Nicoll;
  Heather Walker.
Artists in residence 1983: Richard Kline;
  Frances Walker; David Walker Barker.
Students 1983
  Duncan of Jordanstone: Philip Berjzuck; Karen Guy;
  Sandy Guy.
  Edinburgh College of Art: Wendy McMurdo;
  John Nichol; Mary Scott.
  Glasgow School of Art: Stephen Barclay;
  Simon Brown.
  Gray's School of Art: Callum Innes; Elspeth Roberts;
  Carol Robertson.
Artists in residence 1984: Neil Dallas Brown;
  Tony Stevens.
Students 1984
  Edinburgh College of Art: Rhona A. MacBeth.
  Glasgow School of Art: Rosemary Beaton; Julie Bills;
  Mark Campbell; Sally Carlaw; Kevin McGoldrick.
  Gray's School of Art: Jim Boon.
Artists in residence 1985: Robert McGilvray;
  Barry Nemett.
Students 1985
  Duncan of Jordanstone: Derrick Guild.

Glasgow School of Art: Lorraine Cottrell;
Fiona Robertson; Lorraine Turley.
Artists in residence 1986: Dennis Buchan;
  Paul Huxley; Martin Prekop.
Students 1986
  Duncan of Jordanstone: Angus McEwan; Jacqui
  Nixon; Ian Ritchie.
  Edinburgh College of Art: Moira Bertram.
  Glasgow School of Art: Kirstie Cohen; Sasha Fligel.
  Gray's School of Art: Hugh Gilmour.
Artists in residence 1987: Peter Griffin;
  Kate Whiteford.
Students 1987
  Duncan of Jordanstone: Thomas Crooks; Jon Hunter;
  D. McPhie.
  Edinburgh College of Art: George Glen;
  Lynn McGregor; Ross Thomson.
  Glasgow School of Art: Fiona Cunningham;
  Alexander Dempster; Edward Stewart.
  Gray's School of Art: Nelson Diplexcito; Joe Fan;
  Fiona Hamilton.
Artists in residence 1988: Geoffrey Brunell;
  Phil Hanson.
Students 1988
  Duncan of Jordanstone: Stuart Gilmour; Nael Hanna;
  Alison Murdoch.
  Edinburgh College of Art: John Brown;
  Linda Hennikor; Andrew Parkinson.
  Glasgow School of Art: Debbie Lee;
  Pervase Mohammed; Brian Smithe Smillie.
  Gray's School of Art: Helen Keran; Susan Matt;
  Thomas Tait.
Artists in residence 1989: Judy Geichman;
  Frank Piateck.
Students 1989
  Duncan of Jordanstone: Louise Ritchie; Karen Robbie;
  Lorna Robertson.
  Edinburgh College of Art: Steven Brake;
  Fiona Hamilton; Alison Philp.
  Glasgow School of Art: Julie Bolton; Alison Chisholm;
  Sharon Goodlet.

Gray's School of Art: Brian Gibson; Dougal McKenzie;
Heather Jo Wade.
Artists in residence 1990:
  Jeffrey Mongrain; Ed Shay.
Students 1990
  Duncan of Jordanstone: Helen McAllister;
  Ian Sturrock.
  Edinburgh College of Art: Allan Fenemore;
  Shona Macdonald.
  Glasgow School of Art: Susan Steele.
  Gray's School of Art: Neil Gall; Edward Soutar.
Artists in residence 1991:
  Susanna Coffey; Douglas Thomson.
Students 1991
  Duncan of Jordanstone: Jill Farquhar;
  Eoghann McColl.
  Edinburgh College of Art: Marianne Dey;
  Ewan Robertson.
  Glasgow School of Art: Stewart Buchanan;
  Catherine Cowern.
  Gray's School of Art: Anna Boggon; Mark Scadding.
Artists in residence 1992:
  Peter Bevan; Susan Kraut; Martin Prekop.
Students 1992
  Duncan of Jordanstone: Elaine Fraser;
  Dion Treverethan.
  Edinburgh College of Art: Tomas Lewis;
  Susan McMahon.
  Glasgow School of Art: Lee Martin; Jane Shanks.
  Gray's School of Art: Claire Broadfoot;
  Neil McIvor.
Artists in residence 1993:
  Michiko Itatani; Evelien Nijeboer;
  Douglas Thomson.
Students 1993
  Duncan of Jordanstone: Melanie Stokes;
  Cordelia Underhill.
  Edinburgh College of Art: Jane Benson;
  Kristin Mojsiewicz.
  Glasgow School of Art: Martin Fowler.
  Gray's School of Art: Kate Frame; Judith Hay.

Index